INSPIRED STORIES

50 Years of Answered Prayer

VOLUME 1

COMPILED BY

JOHN D. BECKETT & DAVE KUBAL

PROCLAMATION HOUSE

Heralding faith and freedom to the generations.

Unless otherwise indicated, all Scripture quotations are from The ESV® Bible (The Holy Bible, English Standard Version®), copyright © 2001 by Crossway, a publishing ministry of Good News Publishers. Used by permission. All rights reserved. Scripture quotations noted K21 are taken from the 21st Century King James Version®, copyright © 1994. Used by permission of Deuel Enterprises, Inc., Gary, SD 57237. All rights reserved. Scripture quotations marked (NLT) are taken from the Holy Bible, New Living Translation, copyright ©1996, 2004, 2015 by Tyndale House Foundation. Used by permission of Tyndale House Publishers, Carol Stream, Illinois 60188. All rights reserved. Scripture quotations marked (NIV) are taken from the Holy Bible, New International Version®, NIV®. Copyright © 1973, 1978, 1984, 2011 by Biblica, Inc.™ Used by permission of Zondervan. All rights reserved worldwide. www.zondervan.comThe "NIV" and "New International Version" are trademarks registered in the United States Patent and Trademark Office by Biblica, Inc.™

ISBN: 978-1-7379016-4-8

Printed in the United States of America

Published by
Proclamation House, Inc.
6 Main St. Ext #3554, Plymouth, MA 02361
www.ProclamationHouse.org

PROCLAMATION HOUSE
Heralding faith and freedom to the generations.

This book is dedicated to every intercessor for America. Your prayers have made, are making, and will continue to make a difference. We honor you.

And when he had taken the scroll, the four living creatures and the twenty-four elders fell down before the Lamb, each holding a harp, and golden bowls full of incense, which are the prayers of the saints.... "To him who sits on the throne and to the Lamb be blessing and honor and glory and might forever and ever!" (Rev. 5:8, 13)

CONTENTS:

PART 4: POWERFUL PRAYER WARRIORS

FOREWORD

Answered prayer is the strongest catalyst to boldly engaging your next prayer assignment. Yet, we often come at prayer, unlike other endeavors, with lowered expectations. By contrast:

- the researcher, who fully expects tangible results from his or her inquiry.
- the teacher, who assesses a student's learning from specific test outcomes.
- the investor, who gauges financial decisions by results-driven performance.

But prayer? Answers can seem elusive.

For a moment, pause and consider: When did you last see your prayer answered? As you recall this, can you sense again that special joy — my prayer mattered! There you are! You have your very own "memorial stone" marking the occasion. You are once again reassured that God is nearer than you may have supposed, and that the answers to your prayers are indeed being mysteriously worked out.

I have found that memorial stones are precious to me. One such was laid at a prayer conference held in Singapore in the late 1980s. A representative from Nepal described some intense bondage within her country. One result was that Christians had great difficulty reaching the Nepalese with the gospel. "We can count on two hands the number of believers in the entire country," she said. "We believe a spiritual force holds us captive, and that force is represented by the goddess Kali. In fact, a statue to that goddess is featured in the center of Katmandu, our capital. It depicts the goddess' feet standing atop the writhing figures of prostrate men. The intent is the suppression of every man in our nation."

God gave faith to our small group to take authority over that evil spiritual power — a large, even risky undertaking that is not recommended apart from the Spirit's clear direction. But this was the right time and the right group, and we sensed God's leading. Powerfully, and specifically, we took spiritual authority over that wicked spiritual force. It seemed to us that heaven was thundering! Though we believed we'd "broken through," full validation came some years later as we learned that not only were multitudes coming to the Lord, but Nepal had become a sending country, taking the gospel out to surrounding regions. God heard our prayer!

"God intends prayer to have an answer," wrote Andrew Murray. In the early 1900s, he gave direction and depth to the prayer lives of many. His works continue to inspire. In his preface to the book *With Christ in the School of Prayer,* he says: "The Father waits to hear every prayer of faith. He wants to give us whatever we ask for in Jesus' name. God intends prayer to have an answer, and no one has yet fully conceived what God will do for the child who believes that his prayer will be heard. God hears prayers."

Inspired Stories is a labor of love by the staff of Intercessors for America. It may be your faith-building gateway to more effective prayer. Curated from IFA's 50 years of encouraging effective prayer and, where possible, reporting the answers, this new publication is unique. In it you will find insights that will inspire and strengthen your personal prayer life. These are the stories of everyday folks like you and me: carpenters and homemakers; young and old; theologically adept, and new believers.

Each of these stories encouraged me, challenged me to pray, and made me think of other examples. Vast is the tapestry God is weaving of answers to faith-filled prayers. Every chapter — and they are inspired — concludes with an opportunity to engage, to let the experience of others propel you toward your next prayer assignment. That assignment is waiting, with victory, your memorial stone, right around the corner.

As one who was privileged to be there at the beginning of IFA in 1973, I have been able to witness firsthand God's faithfulness, and that of numerous dedicated staff over the years, bringing us to this milestone. The mission is not completed. In fact, the need has never been greater as we approach the day of the Lord's return. Thank you for your part, as you persevere in faith and in prayer.

— John D. Beckett
Co-Founder and Board Member
Intercessors for America

INTRODUCTION

For our struggle is not against flesh and blood, but against the rulers, against the authorities, against the powers of this dark world and against the spiritual forces of evil in the heavenly realms
(Ephesians 6:12 NIV).

This well-known verse describes the spiritual reality we're seeing in our lives and in our nation.

In 1973, a group of leaders understood this reality and called a nation to prayer. Intercessors for America (IFA) began. For 50 years, a growing number of Christians have joined together through this organization to pray for our nation.

But national and governmental intercession is a marathon, not a sprint. Yes, there are times when the wind is at your back and you feel light on your feet. Other times, your legs feel heavy and are slow to move. Sometimes the wind and even rain oppose you.

When I took the helm of IFA in 2008, the economic recession that gripped the nation was a physical manifestation of the malaise of the Church. Our government opposed the things of God, and people were discouraged. Motivating souls to intercession for the nation was difficult.

Then, in 2016, the Lord began moving upon hundreds of thousands of hearts, burdening them to commit to praying for this nation. There have been great answers to those prayers — and also an emergence of great evils — during this time.

In preparing for the celebration of our 50th anniversary, IFA's staff began doing research in our archives. We've discovered ample evidence that God has truly been answering prayers — in large ways and small, and in good times and bad. We found some stories that made us cry tears of joy, and we came across others that reminded us there's nothing new under the sun.

What you will find in these pages you're holding, and what you will be encouraged by, are the stories of people who were inspired to pray — and the blessed results of their intercession. *Inspired Stories* recounts just a few of the answered-prayer stories from the 50-year history of IFA. We've added engagement questions with each story, for you to reflect on personally or share with a group. It's my own heart's prayer that your faith will be renewed and bolstered by these powerful and true stories that you won't find in today's headlines or in the history books.

— Dave Kubal
President/CEO
Intercessors for America

Then Isaiah the son of Amoz sent to Hezekiah, saying, "Thus says the Lord, the God of Israel: Because you have prayed to me concerning Sennacherib king of Assyria ... " (Isaiah 37:21).

Delight yourself in the Lord, and he will give you the desires of your heart (Psalm 37:4).

"Call to me and I will answer you, and will tell you great and hidden things that you have not known" (Jeremiah 33:3).

PART 1: SHAPING HISTORY THROUGH PRAYER

———◆———

God invites His people to be part of history — to "shape" history, as renowned Bible teacher and IFA co-founder Derek Prince referred to it. This is another way of describing intercessory prayer. God inspires His people to pray, and then He answers those prayers. Once our eyes are opened to this, we see history with new eyes and a fresh perspective. We see God's hand in the headlines and the history books. At the same time, there are some things God does not do unless we pray.

REP. BECKY CURRIE IN FRONT OF THE SUPREME COURT BUILDING IN WASHINGTON, D.

1

THE MOST PRAYED-FOR PERSON IN AMERICA

By Dave Kubal

In 1973 the Roe v. Wade decision made the U.S. one of the most dangerous places in the world for the unborn. This decision catalyzed prayer for the nation and was a major impetus for the birth of Intercessors for America (IFA). From the beginning, IFA acknowledged that abortion violates God's law and started praying for the reversal of Roe.

As I have prayed for the end of abortion on demand in America and led a national network in praying against this great evil, I always had a sense that we were praying for *someone.* I felt that someone would have to set things in motion somehow to spark an end to Roe v. Wade. So, as millions upon millions of us prayed for decades, we were all praying for *someone* to do something. And these were not once-in-a-while prayers; they were daily prayers.

While we were praying for someone through the ups and downs of life, God was answering, orchestrating events, protecting, nudging. This is just the kind of unlikely story that God specializes in.

CURRIE IN HIGH SCHOOL

Becky Currie was a high school sophomore in Mississippi in 1973, participating in her first political campaign, after being encouraged by a female lawyer to get involved in politics.

Some years later, Becky was working her way through nursing school when she was faced with an unplanned pregnancy. Although some were urging her to abort the baby, God captured her heart to protect the life of her unborn daughter. Imagine how all the prayers to save many lives in the aftermath of Roe also saved this one life.

Once she finished nursing school, Becky began working in labor and delivery (which she continues to do today). She still cries tears of joy and appreciation every time a baby is born, a reflection of the heart of God for each life.

As millions prayed for her, she went through many trials in her life, but she always felt God speak to her, even during her days growing up in the Baptist church. Regardless of what she went through, she always felt close to God.

In 2007, she began considering a run for state office. She prayed: "Lord, show me if I should run. If this is of You, let me know." Then, she went knocking on every door across three counties.

She believed that if her election wasn't anointed, it would not happen. As president of IFA, I know how important it is to pray for elected officials. Since the beginning of this organization, we have

CURRIE'S NURSING SCHOOL GRADUATION PICTURE (ABOVE), AND A PHOTO TAKEN AROUND THE TIME SHE DECIDED TO RUN FOR OFFICE IN HER HOME STATE OF MISSISSIPPI (BELOW)

prayed for godly people to win elections and to serve well. How many times has our view of this been shortsighted? I wonder how often our prayers have been answered but we don't know it, because this may involve people like Becky, whose impact isn't recognized for years?

Becky did win election in 2007, and she continues to serve in the Mississippi legislature. Throughout her tenure, she has sponsored a number of bills to protect life. She has always counted on God's voice to direct her.

REP. CURRIE HAS SERVED IN THE MISSISSIPPI HOUSE OF REPRESENTATIVES SINCE 2008 AND IS ALSO A MEMBER OF THE MISSISSIPPI NURSES' ASSOCIATION

In 2016 she wrote and sponsored the Gestational Age Act (GAA). The origins of this particular bill were in a personal experience Becky had as a labor and delivery nurse: She had helped deliver a 15-week-old baby who fought desperately to live. That brave little baby inspired Becky to propose a law that would outlaw abortions after 15 weeks.

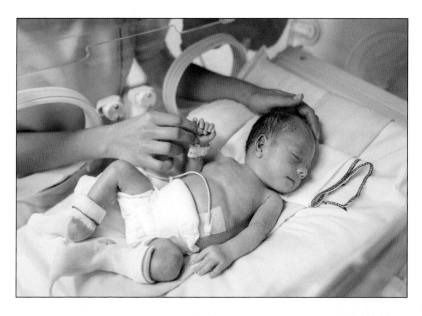

Although Becky had been involved with dozens of pro-life bills, she knew that this particular bill was going to go to the Supreme Court as a challenge to Roe, and so it did. Some may wonder how she knew this. But for a woman who had been tuned to the voice of the Lord since her childhood, it was really not surprising. She had a deep sense that this bill was special, and she was proved right.

TOP LEFT: REP. CURRIE (FAR RIGHT) WATCHES AS MISSISSIPPI GOV. PHIL BRYANT (SEATED) SIGNS THE 2018 GESTATIONAL AGE ACT, WHICH PAVED THE WAY FOR THE OVERTURNING OF ROE V. WADE ON JUNE 24, 2022. TOP RIGHT: PROTESTERS OUTSIDE THE SUPREME COURT BUILDING

The law was challenged by pro-abortion providers in the state, as all pro-life laws are. And it went all the way to the Supreme Court. In the years and months before the oral arguments, the Supreme Court had changed dramatically. Those progressive justices who were determined to keep abortion on demand and to maintain the constitutionally weak Roe decision declined in number, and three new justices came in, all of whom were constitutional originalists and saw clearly the problems with Roe.

On the night before the hearing, I had the great pleasure of meeting Becky, who was honored by IFA at a prayer event. I was so nervous about meeting her. I could feel God's presence upon her, and it was almost like I could feel the millions of prayers offered up for her. I don't know anyone who has been the object of more prayers than Becky.

The rest is history. The hearing went well — though a draft decision was leaked to the press by someone in the court. But finally, on June 24,

IN 2022, REP. CURRIE WAS HONORED FOR HER WORK AUTHORING THE GESTATIONAL AGE ACT, THE STATE LAW THAT LED TO THE EVENTUAL CHALLENGING OF ROE V. WADE. HERE, CURRIE IS PRESENTED WITH A SPECIAL CONGRESSIONAL TRIBUTE BY IFA PRESIDENT AND CEO DAVE KUBAL (LEFT), AND U.S. SEN. CINDY HYDE-SMITH (RIGHT), OF MISSISSIPPI

2022, the legally and morally bankrupt Roe v. Wade decision was overturned by the Supreme Court's ruling in Dobbs v. Jackson.

It has been said that the Dobbs v. Jackson decision overturned Roe v. Wade. But that's not the whole story; God also raised up Becky Currie to overturn Roe, and He raised up hundreds of thousands of intercessors to pray for her. I believe she is the most prayed-for person in the past 50 years of this nation.

ENGAGE:

Your prayers and actions may be having a much greater impact than you imagine. Have you ever considered how your prayers for change in our nation may be critical to the life of a world-changer?

PRESIDENT REAGAN DELIVERS HIS ICONIC SPEECH AT THE BRANDENBURG GATE ON JUNE 12, 1987

2

HOW THE BERLIN WALL *REALLY* CAME DOWN

By Dave Kubal

"Mr. Gorbachev, tear down this wall!"

This iconic line, delivered on June 12, 1987, by the genius communicator President Ronald Reagan, was one of the most effective moments in America's leadership for global freedom. It also represented one of the greatest opportunities that American intercessors ever had to pray down the walls of oppression and totalitarianism in our time — and not just in America, but everywhere around the globe.

President Reagan spoke to the entire world, declaring a policy of freedom. He called upon the general secretary of the Communist Party of the Soviet Union, Mikhail Gorbachev, to tear down the Berlin wall, which had encircled West Berlin and controlled the lives of 2 million people living under the curse of communism.

As it happened, an urgency to pray for change on the other side of the Iron Curtain was then gripping the members of IFA. At an IFA conference a few years earlier, Intercessors for Denmark head Johannes Facius addressed some top priorities for prayer. The first was "that communist world power be broken."

THE CLOSED BRANDENBURG GATE DURING THE PERIOD OF THE BERLIN WALL

American intercessors had no way of knowing then that their prayers for human freedom were actually undergirding a movement overseas — specifically, in East Germany and across the Eastern bloc.

Reagan's speech was strategically delivered in front of the Brandenburg Gate. This beautiful, historic gate was chosen as the backdrop not only because it was part of the Berlin Wall — literally separating people living under military occupation from those living in freedom — but also because the 200-year-old Brandenburg Gate was a symbol of freedom fighters over the centuries.

Though some believe that Reagan's bold command is the reason the wall came down two years later, there is more to the story. For almost 40 years, the Soviet-dominated East German Communist Party had ruled East Germany with an iron fist. Dictator Erich Honecker threatened that death or imprisonment awaited anyone who dared to defy the German Democratic Republic (GDR).

There was a small group of men willing to fight against this force, though perhaps not in the way you would think. In 1982, about five years before Reagan's famous speech and the same year IFA intercessors prayed that the "communist world power be broken," the Rev. Christian Führer and some other pastors started a simple prayer meeting they called Prayers for Peace. Every Monday the faithful would gather, light 40 candles (representing the Israelites' 40 years in the wilderness), and pray for peace in Germany.

For some time, the authorities ignored Pastor Führer and his prayer meetings. Eventually, however, attendance grew into the thousands, and the GDR could no longer turn a blind eye. Spies began infiltrating the meetings and recording the names of those present. Agents of the GDR tried to intimidate Pastor Führer — once even leaving him out in the snow to die. Numerous people who attended the prayer meetings got fired from their jobs, even though the meetings had no political agenda. Young people then took the place of their parents at these prayer meetings, because they had no jobs to lose.

Despite persecution, attendees continued interceding for several years. They saw little by way of tangible answers to prayer during those years. The only "answer" some could point to was Reagan's speech, and even with that, two years had passed and the wall still stood.

Then, on Oct. 9, 1989, Pastor Führer convened the meeting but sensed that the Lord desired they do something different that week as they prayed. Candles were handed out to the attendees, with instructions that they should light their candles, leave the church building, and march peacefully to the center of the city.

The GDR army, meanwhile, hearing that a prayer walk was being organized, mobilized troops and even tanks to line the street leading from the church to the city center.

Knowing they could suffer the loss of their jobs, or even their lives, some 2,000 intercessors courageously emerged from the church, willing to accept any consequences. They were greatly surprised to see that 100,000 candle-carrying Germans had come out in support of their prayer march.

Together, they walked, despite the GDR troops who lined the streets, armed with machine guns and backed by Russian tanks. Never before had the GDR leadership allowed this kind of defiance. Previously, the troops would have shot any such demonstrators.

What happened next is unexplainable in human terms. The demonstrators bravely approached soldiers, who were fellow Germans, and offered them lighted candles. Miraculously, the soldiers began putting down their weapons to receive the candles. Soon, all the soldiers had lowered their guns and joined the protestors. The Russian tanks backed up and returned to the barracks.

BERLINERS TRIUMPHANTLY CELEBRATE THE END OF THE CITY'S WALLED PARTITION

This prayerful demonstration broke the power of communist Russia. It became clear that Honecker's dictatorship could not continue. The following week, Honecker resigned. One month later, the Berlin Wall came down.

In the weeks following Honecker's resignation and after Gorbachev began tearing down the wall, the disgraced GDR leaders publicly admitted this: "We were ready for anything — except candles and prayers."

ENGAGE:

What walls do you see in our national life today that need to come down? Ask God to bring down every wall that must come down — and to inspire us to keep praying with endurance and courage.

PARTICIPANTS IN THE BALTIC CHAIN HOLD CANDLES AND LITHUANIAN FLAGS WITH BLACK RIBBONS IN PROTEST

3

'SUDDENLY' IN THE SOVIET UNION

By Nicole Arnoldbik & Judy McDonough

Prayer was an integral part of the reunification of Germany and a critical part of the collapse of the Soviet Union. Though, looking back, some may say that the end of the Soviet Union was inevitable, that's not the way things seemed at the time, especially not to those living under Soviet rule.

During the fall of 1989, Germans tore down the Berlin Wall; Poland and Hungary installed noncommunist governments; Czechoslovakia was transformed by the peaceful Velvet Revolution; and protests swept the Soviet Union during the Moscow Spring. The first democratically elected legislature met in Moscow in the spring of 1989, heralding the start of something new. In August, some 2 million residents across the USSR formed the Baltic Chain — their linked arms forming a human chain stretching for about 400 miles, from Estonia through Latvia and into Lithuania.

These historic occurrences, now called part of a revolution, seemed to happen suddenly, like the fall of the Berlin Wall. Yet, again like the fall of that wall, these were events that had been bathed in years of prayer.

WENDY AND JOHN BECKETT

For many years, IFA co-founder and board member John Beckett and his wife, Wendy, witnessed firsthand the spiritual underpinnings of the peaceful revolution through close relationships with Russian pastors.

The Becketts visited Moscow to encourage their Russian friends and missionaries several times during this critical era. Freedom was stirring, but the Soviet stronghold was not yet "revolutionized." The rooms in their hotels were bugged, with security personnel and undercover agents always watching their every move.

During one trip, a Russian pastor boldly led a prayer circle in the hotel lobby. The Becketts never forgot his prayer: that the yoke would be lifted from the country. At the prayer's end, Wendy opened her eyes and

THE MOSCOW IZMAILOVO HOTEL COMPLEX IN RUSSIA, WHERE THE BECKETTS STAYED

SOVIET HEAD OF STATE MIKHAIL GORBACHEV (FAR RIGHT) LOOKS ON AS PRESIDENT REAGAN GREETS A BOY DURING A TOUR OF RED SQUARE ON MAY 31, 1988, IN MOSCOW

saw an undercover agent begin walking toward them, then stop suddenly and move away. In an IFA newsletter of that time, John recounts another powerful instance of prayer:

"We sat huddled in a small 16th-floor apartment on Moscow's near north side. The last chair had just been taken. It was Thursday night, and believers were coming together to pray. Some were in their mid-teens, some quite elderly. Pleasantries were brief; then, to prayer. And pray they did, calling out to God in Russian and other tongues. Such earnestness. Such a yearning for the heart of God. This particular evening, it would end early; often the dawn would see them still together, and they would leave directly for work. Now they could come and go without unusual precautions; even a year ago, great care had to be taken, and they would arrive and depart by twos and threes.

"My thoughts keep coming back to the word 'suddenly.' How often it appears in Scripture (read Jeremiah 51:8, and then Revelation 18:10). How often God moved when men least suspected. But always with a purpose.

"Events in Eastern Europe and in the Soviet Union have left us dumbfounded, groping for words. Even a year ago, a person prophesying this would have been scoffed at, his sanity questioned.

A VIEW OF THE MOSCOW KREMLIN WALL AND CATHEDRAL SQUARE

Almost overnight these changes have opened up religious freedom and the availability of the Bible. Shortwave religious broadcasts penetrate the smallest Siberian hamlet. Television and the fax machine are networking freedom movements around the globe. We're seeing those who have suffered for Christ take the gospel out of Russia and East bloc countries."

The freedom stirred and grew, and the need for prayer continued. Four years later, IFA board member Sally Fesperman participated in on-site intercession at the Derek Prince Ministries Conference in Moscow (in May 1993). In partnership with 23 intercessors from the English-speaking world, Sally and her team responded to a call of God to intercede inside the former Soviet Union while 1,000 pastors and leaders gathered from all over the Confederation of Independent States (CIS). She testified to how God moved mightily through His Spirit:

"Many nationalities and many ethnic groups of people were there, but all with one heart for what God wanted to do for the Russian leaders. As a result of the spirit of repentance, there came an outpouring of forgiveness between individual people as well as groups of people. Many [IFA intercessors] may have been among those who prayed for these meetings. … *Now to him who is able to do immeasurably more*

than all we ask or imagine, according to his power that is at work within us, to him be glory in the church and in Christ Jesus throughout all generations, for ever and ever! Amen (Ephesians 3:20–21).

ENGAGE:

What impossible things do we face today, nationally and globally? What injustices, tyrannies, and evils can we bring to the Lord? And how can we intercede for those in the midst of these evils, those who need our prayer support though we may not even know their names?

MARCHING BANDS PERFORM IN FRONT OF THE CAPITOL BUILDING TO CELEBRATE THE AMERICAN BICENTENNIAL

4

TERRORIST PLANS THWARTED

By Nicole Arnoldbik, Jill Cataldo,
& Judy McDonough

In the years and months leading to July 4, 1976, Americans were planning a joyous celebration of the nation's bicentennial. At the same time, terrorist groups were planning to exploit the opportunity for purposes of their own. These terrorists were well organized and well armed, and their intentions were clear: to bomb, to burn, to destroy, and above all to disrupt the July 4 bicentennial celebrations, the Democratic Convention in New York City (July 12–15, 1976), and the Olympic Games in Montreal, Canada (July 17–Aug. 1, 1976).

Dr. William Kintner, a University of Pennsylvania political science professor, testified before Congress on June 18, 1976, in hopes that making these serious terrorist threats public would deter the terrorists from acting. Kintner told Congress: "… [T]here is reason to be concerned that the terrorist elements in our society will find the bicentennial an irresistible attraction — not only because the eyes of the world will be focused on the bicentennial festivities, but also because they regard the celebration itself with consuming hostility, since it stands for everything they are opposed to: freedom."

Extremist groups that hate this country and what it stands for, Kintner said, "have been talking in terms of disrupting, or spoiling, the bicentennial." He gave examples of radical rhetoric that implied and could thus incite violence: "A leader of the Puerto Rican Socialist Party has talked about 'turning the bicentennial upside down.' A leader of the American Indian Movement told a Chicago conference in February of this year: 'When they light the candles on the 200th birthday cake, we will be there to blow them out.' The terrorist Weather Underground has talked about 'bringing the fireworks,' and this slogan has been repeated by some of those in charge of a planned mass demonstration in Philadelphia."

PRESIDENT GERALD FORD AND FIRST LADY BETTY FORD OBSERVE THE BICENTENNIAL FIREWORKS DISPLAY FROM THE TRUMAN BALCONY AT THE WHITE HOUSE

Radical domestic groups and communist leaders were identified as among those giving rise to the terror threat during the summer of 1976. This coalition of Marxist-Leninist terrorists also included the Native American Solidarity Committee, the Communist Party USA, and many others.

But God raised up His standard, and Satan's plans were stopped cold.

DR. JAMES RHOADS OF THE NATIONAL ARCHIVES CUTS A BIRTHDAY CAKE TO MARK THE 200TH ANNIVERSARY OF THE SIGNING OF THE DECLARATION OF INDEPENDENCE

All three events went ahead, free from any terrorist interference. Prayer was the key here, and so the warfare that did take place was all in the spiritual realm. One example was Joy Dawson's prayer of intercession at a conference in Pittsburgh. As this leader of the Youth With A Mission ministry team began praying, thousands joined her in taking authority over the unseen forces in the heavenlies. Here are excerpts from that powerful prayer:

"... [C]lothed in the armor of God now, we come to address Satan, principalities, and demon powers, and we come to tell you, God the Holy Ghost has disclosed your plans for riots on July 4 in Philadelphia and on into Montreal. ... You will not win, and we come to do aggressive warfare against you in the name of the Lord Jesus and in the power of the Holy Ghost.

"Tonight, I come and address the particular principalities that Satan has allotted to be loosed on July 4. The Holy Ghost has named them to me. They are the principality of lawlessness, the principality of anarchy, and the principality of rebellion — and I tell you right now, you will not do anything to discredit the work of the Living God. I bind you right now.

IN A CEREMONY HELD INSIDE THE CAPITOL ROTUNDA IN WASHINGTON, D.C., MEMBERS OF GREAT BRITAIN'S HOUSE OF LORDS LENT THE MAGNA CARTA TO THE UNITED STATES IN CELEBRATION OF AMERICA'S BICENTENNIAL

I resist you right now. I command you three principalities, in the mighty name of the Lord Jesus, to cease all plans right now. I command confusion in the committees of hell tonight, through Jesus Christ. You will not work, you will not thwart the will of God, because it is written in the word of God: I will work, says the Living God. …

"And we now say to You, O God, as we take our place, having turned from the powers of darkness — we say thanks be unto God who gives us the victory through our Lord Jesus Christ, for we are more than conquerors through Him who washed us in His own precious blood. We praise You now in faith. King God, we worship You and praise You tonight for the sheer privilege of being on the winning side. We worship You because You're the mighty conquering king, the Alpha and Omega, the Beginning and the End, the King of kings, the Lord of lords, the wonderful Lord Jesus Christ. And we tell you tonight that it is a privilege to obey You. We will say 'Yes, Sir!' to anything You ask us to do, and we thank You that Your truth is marching on, because You are marching on. Hallelujah!"

ENGAGE:

*What dangers are you aware the Lord has protected us from?
Give God the praise — out loud. Do you have the faith and
wisdom to passionately pray these kinds of prayers that demolish
strongholds through the power of Jesus Christ?*

5

THE TIMELY BIRTH OF INTERCESSORS FOR UKRAINE

By Dave Kubal

Throughout my tenure as CEO and president of IFA, I have attended the annual National Prayer Breakfast, in Washington, which brings together leaders from around the world for a single purpose: to appeal to heaven. In 2020, I met two men from Ukraine at this event, and we immediately connected.

At that time, the media reported constantly on a false allegation that President Trump had a "quid pro quo" with Ukraine. These men, Maksym Bilousov and Vitaliy Orlov, told me about the real quid pro quo: that the Obama administration, through then–Vice President Biden and others, had refused U.S. aid to Ukraine unless that country adopted America's progressive morality regarding abortion and LGBTQ policies. I was fascinated and saw the hand of God in the revelation of this "intercessory intel."

Maksym and Vitaliy asked me to share wisdom and insight for developing a prayer ministry within their country that would be similar to IFA, and thus, Intercessors for Ukraine was born. Using our website and web designers, they created a powerful online prayer presence for Ukraine. IFA intercessors generously contributed enough to support the effort, from its launch on through the first two years.

PRESIDENT TRUMP SPEAKING AT THE 2020 PRAYER BREAKFAST IN WASHINGTON, D.C.

God knew that this relationship between IFA and IFU would provide the means for critical support and help to Ukraine during the Russian invasion and resultant war. In February 2022, another National Prayer Breakfast was held, and I met again with Vitaliy in Washington, while Maksym stayed in Ukraine. This was one week before Russia invaded. IFA staff members joined hundreds of U.S., Ukrainian, and Ukrainian-American leaders at a separate prayer breakfast. Everyone felt the importance of our prayers at that moment in history.

DAVE KUBAL AND OTHER VOLUNTEERS PACK UKRAINE MEALS IN FLORIDA

When Russia invaded, IFA was perfectly poised by the hand of God to help spearhead the efforts of UkraineMeals.com. In a matter of days, a small coalition of nonprofits, including IFA, raised funds for 1 million meals. Within a week, those meals were packed and on their way to Poland. Distribution into Ukraine was trickier, because tractor-trailers were being targeted by Russian warplanes. Generous donations covered the purchase of minivans

GOSPEL BOOKLETS ARE GIVEN OUT WITH UKRAINE MEALS

to safely transport the food throughout Ukraine. These efforts fed not only bodies, but souls as well.

The invasion stirred the people of Ukraine to an incredible openness to the gospel and to prayer. Special funding through IFA helped IFU print and distribute more than 300,000 prayer guides to Ukrainians. At the time of this printing, more than 3 million meals have been sent, and IFU has shared the gospel with 1 million Ukrainians. At another prayer breakfast, one year after the start of the war, officials from Ukraine were eager to tell IFA how grateful they were for the meals. With the bombings destroying the electrical grid, these ready-to-eat meals provided food regardless of any absence of the means of cooking.

IFU was also able to post on billboards some uplifting messages showing how devoted many of the Ukrainians are to God. Many turned to God in the midst of the war.

MAKSYM BILOUSOV STANDS WITH HIS DAUGHTER BY A GOD-HONORING BILLBOARD IN UKRAINE THAT SAYS: 'WITH GOD, WE WILL WIN!'

The special relationship with IFU also provided IFA a front-row seat to witness answered prayer and miracles. One of the members of Vitaliy's church who serves in the military called his parents from the front line to tell them that military intelligence had warned of a large drop of Russian paratroopers near where he was stationed. His commanding officers told him, "Expect it." He called to ask his parents to pray and get others to pray, which they did.

The Russian planes did fly overhead, and the paratroopers began dropping from the sky. But something else happened. "God sent a strong wind," Vitaliy told us. That wind pushed the Russian paratroopers back over the line, into Russian territory!

One of Maksym's pastoral assistants, Vladimir, joined the army. He held small church services daily, and everyone in the unit except for one man attended. Another man, in a time of peril for the unit, asked Vladimir: "Can you lead me in the sinner's prayer? I need that stuff."

God used American intercessors, their hearts knit together in advance of war, to encourage, undergird, and provide for brothers and sisters in Christ far across the globe. This strong relationship continues to this day.

TOP (LEFT): MAKSYM, VITALIY, DAVE, AND KRIS KUBAL MEET IN LEESBURG, VA.; TOP (RIGHT): MAKSYM'S CHURCH CARES FOR PEOPLE FLEEING UKRAINE; BOTTOM (LEFT): VITALIY, ALONG WITH HIS WIFE AND SON, MEET WITH IVANKA TRUMP THROUGH UKRAINEMEALS.ORG; BOTTOM (RIGHT): MAKSYM WITH TWO UKRAINIAN REFUGEES

ENGAGE:

Through all of this, God has worked in ways we could never have planned or imagined. Take time to remember and to record the miracles in your own life as an encouragement for yourself and others.

U.S. SOLDIERS GUARD THE TARMAC AT KARZAI INTERNATIONAL AIRPORT, AFGHANISTAN, IN AUGUST 2021

6

SAVING AZIZ – AND MANY OTHERS

By Judy McDonough

In August 2022, thousands of people were at risk following the disastrous U.S. pullout from Afghanistan. Early in the crisis, Danielle posted this on IFApray.org:

> *It's easy to hear Abba's heart through the pen of IFA intercessors leaving comments at IFApray.org. IFA is a never-ending source of encouragement and truth. The situation in Afghanistan has left me breathless and in tears over the losses experienced. I love how the Lord has encouraged us that **we just haven't heard the stories yet!** Intercessors understand the depth of heaviness with not only this situation but also the effort to systematically dismantle our God-given republic. God forgive us; God deliver us from our Enemy. We know all things are in Your holy, righteous, justice-filled hands. We just want to be in the gap doing our part when we see You.*

God heard and answered, using IFA to do it.

IFA Chief Program Officer Kris Kubal served on a committee praying for persecuted Christians. Also on that committee was Lt. Col. Tommy Waller, a Marine officer involved at a high level in national security challenges. He asked Kris if IFA would pray in advance of a series of vital meetings.

LT. COL. TOMMY WALLER AT AN IFA EVENT

These meetings were of the level and type that impact all of us, yet only a few people knew anything about them. Kris made sure IFA published confidential and urgent calls for prayer. God answered. There was a shift in this series of meetings, which Waller could attribute only to a supernatural move of God.

Fast-forward to the Afghanistan pullout and the humanitarian crisis that followed. Since Waller had witnessed firsthand the power of prayer and the responsiveness of IFA to pray when asked, he again reached out on behalf of a colleague who was organizing the rescue of Americans and of Afghan allies marked for execution because they had assisted

TROOPS STAND GUARD WHILE REFUGEES BOARD BUSES

America. This colleague was Chad Robichaux, founder of Mighty Oaks Foundation and a co-founder of Save Our Allies.

Robichaux, a decorated Force Reconnaissance Marine and a mixed-martial-arts star, told the story on an IFA webcast and in his book, *Saving Aziz*. Humanly speaking, the rescue mission was impossible. Diplomacy involving multiple nations, very real dangers on the ground in Afghanistan, and tactical and logistical challenges all made any success a long shot.

IFA received near-real-time prayer requests, and answers to prayer came just as fast. Robichaux intended to save one family: his former translator Aziz and his wife and children. The first miracle is that this mission resulted in the rescue of Aziz, his family, as well as 17,000 Afghanistans who were marked for death because they had aided the U.S. during the 20-year occupation.

Having witnessed firsthand the danger that so many Afghans faced after the U.S. withdrawal, Robichaux wanted to do more. He headed back to Afghanistan to create escape routes through Tajikistan, an area crawling with Russian and Chinese

CHAD ROBICHAUX (TOP), USMC FORCE RECON VETERAN, FOUNDER OF THE MIGHTY OAKS FOUNDATION, AND AUTHOR OF *SAVING AZIZ* (MIDDLE); AZIZ AND HIS FAMILY (RIGHT) AFTER ARRIVING SAFELY IN THE UNITED STATES

THE PANJ RIVER, WHICH SERVES AS A BORDER BETWEEN TAJIKISTAN AND AFGHANISTAN

forces. On the flight over, Robichaux was uncharacteristically gripped with fear. He reached out through Waller for prayer from IFA. An urgent request was immediately published on the website. Untold thousands in the IFA community went to prayer. Robichaux was then overcome with a peace that persisted throughout the perilous mission.

Intercessors are not often on the frontlines physically, but by serving courageously on the frontlines spiritually, they always support those who are.

ENGAGE:

Intercessors are often called the special-operations forces of prayer. How can Robichaux's story empower your intercessions in ways you've not experienced before?

A MAN RAISES HIS HANDS IN PRAYER OUTSIDE THE U.S. SUPREME COURT, IN WASHINGTON, D.C.

7

ASSASSINATION PLAN SUPERNATURALLY STOPPED

By Dave Kubal

When the Supreme Court agreed to hear the Dobbs v. Jackson Women's Health Organization decision on abortion, I knew that the Lord wanted IFA to become involved. This case out of Mississippi seemed different from many others that had gone before. I believe we were inspired by the Holy Spirit to submit an amicus (friend of the court) brief that included a prayer people could sign. I thought it would be incredible for our prayers to be part of the Supreme Court record in the case. We connected with Christian attorneys who had been praying and waiting for an organization courageous enough to submit a brief that outlined how the Supreme Court's abortion decisions over these 50 years had set our nation up for judgment. Since that lined up with Scripture and they liked our idea about the prayer, we filed this unique brief together.

The next step was a prayer initiative: daily prayer for the justices, for the lawyers on both sides, and for the justices' clerks. For months, intercessors prayed for the justices and the lawyers by name. There were many, many prayer initiatives by many organizations. At the same time, I don't know of any others that prayed for the justices' clerks by name.

Oral arguments took place on Dec. 1, 2021, and the nation waited for the decision, expecting an announcement in June. On May 2, 2022, something happened that was utterly unprecedented: The draft opinion was leaked to the press. The opinion outlined the overturning of Roe v. Wade. We don't know who leaked it, but we know now that it was someone from inside the court. Was it a clerk? How was he or she impacted by our prayers? We know it's no coincidence that we had been covering these people in prayer. And those prayers became even more important.

The public response to the leak was extreme. On one side were those who have long fought and prayed for life and against the legally incorrect Roe decision. On the other side were abortion activists, people who were confused, and people who were enraged. Justice Alito has said publicly many times that he believes the leak put the lives of those justices in the decision's majority at risk. And since it was not yet a finalized decision, the death of any one of those justices could have changed the result.

POLICE OFFICERS WATCH AS ABORTION-RIGHTS ADVOCATES DEMONSTRATE OUTSIDE THE HOME OF JUSTICE KAVANAUGH ON MAY 18, 2022, IN CHEVY CHASE, MARYLAND

Protests erupted outside the homes of all the justices in the majority. Despite state laws that should have been enforced, the protesters carried explicit signs, shouted, and wrote horrible things in chalk on the sidewalks and streets of the neighborhoods where the justices lived. No Supreme Court justices or their families had ever experienced this kind of pressure or these sorts of fear tactics at their homes. Even worse, three of these justices had young children at home.

The leak of the Dobbs draft opinion, and the nation's response to it, impressed once again upon intercessors nationwide the urgency of persistent prayers for protection, especially for those five justices who supported the overturn of Roe. The answer to these prayers was dramatic.

Nicholas Roske was very angry about the possibility of abortion laws changing. He was also upset about the May 24, 2022, school massacre in Uvalde, Texas, and concerned about the possible loosening of gun control in a case the Supreme Court would be ruling on.

(FROM LEFT): CHIEF JUSTICE JOHN ROBERTS, ASSOCIATE JUSTICE ELENA KAGAN, ASSOCIATE JUSTICE BRETT KAVANAUGH, AND ASSOCIATE JUSTICE AMY CONEY BARRETT

Roske decided to act on his obsessions.

He purchased a Glock 17 pistol and packed it up along with some ammunition, two gun magazines, a speed loader, a tactical knife, pepper spray, zip ties, and some tools: a nail punch, a hammer, a screwdriver, and a crowbar.

Armed with these, Roske flew from California to Washington, D.C., his intent being to assassinate Justice Brett Kavanaugh.

Roske was upset about a school shooting and brooding over the possibility of relaxed gun control — yet he purchased a gun so that he could himself go out and murder a man. Clearly, he was incited and motivated by the world (incendiary rhetoric broadcast all over the internet and the media), sin, and Satan.

On June 8, 2022, Roske got out of a taxi in front of Justice Kavanaugh's house. He spotted some U.S. marshals by the house and proceeded down the street. Then he texted his sister and phoned 911. He told the operator that he was having suicidal thoughts, that he had a gun, and that he planned to kill the justice.

Miraculously, Roske was soon apprehended by local police without incident. Later investigation revealed that Roske had sent this message on the social gaming platform Discord: "I am shooting for 3" — indicating that assassinating two other justices may have been part of his plan. It seems this man was being demonically led to first kill

A STATUE TITLED *CONTEMPLATION OF JUSTICE* SITS BELOW THE INSCRIPTION OF "EQUAL JUSTICE UNDER LAW" AT THE ENTRANCE TO THE UNITED STATES SUPREME COURT BUILDING

Kavanaugh, perhaps other justices, and then himself. It must have been divine intervention that stopped Roske at the last minute.

We don't always know what effect our prayers are having. In this instance, there may have been further plans for evil that were stopped by the power of prayer. We do know that this particular plan for harm was inexplicably thwarted by a supernatural intervention of God.

ENGAGE:

Pray for spiritual and physical protection over our judges and Supreme Court justices and their families. And write to these judges for whom you intercede, to encourage them and let them know you are praying for them and their decisions, for their safety, and for their loved ones.

OPPOSITE *CONTEMPLATION OF JUSTICE* IS THE FIGURE TITLED *AUTHORITY OF LAW*

> *Lord, it grieves my heart to think of the millions of lives lost because of legal abortion; each life is precious in Your sight, woven together in the womb. We ask that You would forgive us of this national sin and cause the U.S. Supreme Court Justices to agree with You that life is precious. We deserve judgment, but we humbly ask for the wisdom of heaven to bring godly conviction upon our nine Supreme Court Justices. Lord, cause them to rule in favor of protecting life. Lord, we appeal to You as we appeal for life. In Jesus' name. Amen.*

- A PRAYER CONTAINED IN THE AMICUS BRIEF FILED
BY IFA BEFORE THE SUPREME COURT

"Again I say to you, if two of you agree on earth about anything they ask, it will be done for them by my Father in heaven. For where two or three are gathered in my name, there am I among them" (Matthew 18:19–20).

First of all, then, I urge that supplications, prayers, intercessions, and thanksgivings be made for all people, for kings and all who are in high positions, that we may lead a peaceful and quiet life, godly and dignified in every way. This is good, and it is pleasing in the sight of God our Savior ... (1 Timothy 2:1–3).

PART 2:
PRAYING 'ON-SITE' WITH INSIGHT

———◆———

Throughout the past 50 years, the ministry of Intercessors for America has witnessed miracles not only at the national level, but also in states and communities. We have seen that intercessors who pray in and for a particular location have greater insight on how to pray, and that their prayers are often more effective. Communities have thus been transformed, and sometimes this starts with just one or two people praying.

AUTUMN LEAVES DECORATE THE NORTH COAST INLAND TRAIL, IN ELYRIA, OHIO

8

A HOMETOWN VICTORY

By John D. Beckett

In November 1982, our local newspaper announced the intentions of a man we will call Mr. Harris to open an abortion clinic in our area. We couldn't let this threat on our own doorstep go unchallenged.

Within days of the announcement, community and ministry leaders gathered to pray and seek God's wisdom for a plan of action. Present were evangelical ministers, Catholic priests, businessmen, educators, right-to-life representatives, and two outstanding attorneys affiliated with Cleveland-based Lawyers for Life.

Our attorneys, serving on a no-cost basis, gave us counsel we did not want to hear: There was no way to legally prevent the opening of an abortion clinic. They normally don't need permits or licenses, only zoning suitable for medical clinics. "Our fight will not be a legal one," they said, but rather an effort to shape public opinion.

With amazing speed and unity, a strategy was developed to:

- educate the community on the abortion issue, especially elected officials and educators;
- help us understand our legal options and strengthen local codes and ordinances;
- build a prayer network;
- form an intelligence-gathering network for learning about the motivations and strategies of clinic backers;
- encourage alternatives to abortion;
- build strong relationships among pro-life leaders;
- establish a leadership structure with people responsible for each functional area, plus a communications network among those leaders.

At two-to-three-week intervals, our group gathered and new people were added. We purposely kept a low profile as a group to avoid premature publicity. We kept organizational structure to a minimum, although we did settle on a name for our group: Coalition for Life.

We all seemed to sense a total dependence on God, especially as we realized how fully the clinic operators have the law on their side. We were helpless in our own strength. Each meeting began with a time of seeking the Lord, and even though most of us had not known each other previously, the Spirit began knitting us together in a beautiful way.

Several area churches established prayer groups to focus on this threat to our community. A frequent emphasis in our times of prayer was that we might understand more of the character of Harris, the man who wanted to establish the clinic, and that God would lead him to repentance and salvation.

JOHN AND WENDY BECKETT

A 1983 NEWSPAPER CLIPPING SHOWS THE BILLBOARDS SPONSORED BY COALITION FOR LIFE IN OPPOSITION TO THE OPENING OF ABORTION CLINICS IN ELYRIA, OHIO SWAY PUBLIC OPINION AGAINST ABORTION CLINICS OPENING IN ELYRIA, OHIO

By our third meeting, significant momentum was developing. People were writing letters to the editor. Billboard space was reserved for use with the IFA poster that read: All Human Life Is Precious, Including the Unborn. To add emphasis to our local concern, the words NO ABORTION CLINICS HERE were emblazoned across the bottom of the poster. We agreed to show *Assignment of Life*, an excellent pro-life documentary, on a local cable TV station. But in the course of that third meeting, a most remarkable event occurred.

God Intervenes

A Christian businessman in attendance revealed that he felt the Lord wanted him to join us and to share something that had happened three weeks earlier. He said:

"I'm not proud of this, but several years ago, I was a close personal friend of Harris, close enough to be best man at his wedding. We did a lot of partying and other things that weren't very nice as I look back on them.

"Then I met the Lord, and He required me to break off several 'friendships,' including Harris. I hadn't heard from the man in over two years until three weeks ago. When Harris called, it was to talk about a

Elyria ponders abortion rules

By DEBBIE COURTRIGHT
C-T Staff Writer

ELYRIA — After hearing from both pro-life and pro-choice supporters, City Council tonight will come to grips with legislation to regulate abortions performed in Elyria.

So far, petitions have been received from several area church groups protesting abortions in the county. At a Community Development Committee meeting March 10, the Coalition

THE FIGHT TO STOP ABORTION CLINICS GAINED NATIONAL ATTENTION: NBC TV CREWS COVERED THE EVENT, AND CLIPS AIRED ON NATIONAL NEWS AND NBC'S *TODAY* SHOW

real-estate deal, but without prompting on my part, he began to tell me about his plans for an abortion clinic in your area."

Our visitor went on to disclose to us in amazing detail not only Harris' plans, but also what he is like. He said: *"Harris has set up clinics all over the country and has made a fortune from them. He uses outside money, sets up the doctors, uses professional managers, buys the equipment and will get a clinic operating in less than a week to avoid controversy and publicity. He is well organized. He wants a good-looking building, well-groomed in a secure, safe location. He wants it to look respectable and professional."*

To add emphasis, the gentleman said: *"Harris is a lonely, sad person who doesn't like publicity such as letters and billboards. He will avoid coming into an area if there is 'smoke.' He doesn't like paying money, especially to attorneys. Make him know he will have to spend money before he comes in, and it will discourage him. He'll go somewhere else to stay out of court. Once he is set up, he will stay and fight and make his money before you can get him out."*

A Platform for Action

This information gave us great incentive. Not only were we given clear direction to be bold and make this an open, public issue, but we were overwhelmed with the dramatic way in which God had answered our prayer. We sensed that we were truly in the right place at the right time and that He was leading us!

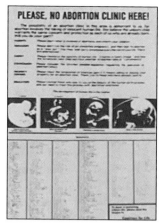

PETITIONS CIRCULATED BY COALITION FOR LIFE WERE DELIVERED TO THE CITY COUNCIL

Our activity intensified in several ways:

- Mailings of pro-life material were made to pastors, high school principals, teachers (approximately 200), and school counselors;
- More churches committed themselves to prayer, bringing the total to 15;
- A local Lutheran church began a pregnancy counseling ministry that included provision of temporary housing with a Christian family for unmarried pregnant women;
- We ran a full-page ad in local newspapers, sponsored by over 500 locals, with appeals to parents, teens, educators, legislators, and clergy to get involved in protecting unborn life. Some $3,000 in revenue was generated from this project;
- We wrote to Harris, including sending copies of news clippings and informing him of our resolute opposition, but also explaining that we were praying regularly for him;
- A slideshow with a message on the need to regulate abortion clinics was prepared and presented to local city councils and committees;
- A computerized mailing list with the names of nearly 800 supporters was developed.

The Council Vote

Without doubt, our greatest triumph in the six-month drama came in April, when the city of Elyria decided to enact legislation regulating abortion clinics. An ordinance was drafted by Lawyers for Life, based on the Akron ordinance but modified to eliminate provisions that had been ruled unconstitutional in the courts. This was the strongest ordinance that we felt could withstand any legal challenge. The city solicitor presented the ordinance, practically verbatim, to the Council.

The air was electric in the Council chambers that night. We will never forget the sight of an overflow crowd of 200 pro-lifers under the spotlights of NBC's TV crew from Cleveland. (Highlights were aired in the news that night and on the *Today* show the next morning.) Even two women who had

DURING THE PUBLIC HEARINGS, MANY ATTENDEES WEPT AS ABORTION METHODS WERE DESCRIBED

come to oppose the ordinance got caught up in the inspired testimony of those in support of the legislation and ended up siding with us. The momentum was heightened further as one council member after another and then the mayor all spoke in opposition to abortion and in support of the ordinance.

A UNANIMOUS AFFIRMATIVE VOTE BROUGHT SUPPORTERS TO THEIR FEET IN APPLAUSE AND GRATITUDE FOR THE CITY COUNCIL'S DECISION FAVORING A PRO-LIFE ORDINANCE

The unanimous affirmative vote brought us all to our feet in applause and gratitude for the Council, which acted with great conviction and courage.

Especially precious was our Coalition for Life meeting later in the week, in which the members of our diverse little band of citizens bowed their heads and hearts for at least 20 minutes, giving thanks and praise to a wonderful God who blesses so richly, and praying again for Harris and for others like him who are caught in such deception.

We know the battle isn't won. Even the ordinance is but a small step toward the paramount need in America today: to stop the shedding of innocent blood. But it reaffirmed how much God wants to lead us, and how He will act supernaturally on our behalf if we let Him. To Him be all the praise!

ENGAGE:

Seek the Lord about the needs and problems in your community. Pray for your community leaders to seek divine wisdom and direction.

9

MISSISSIPPI *TURNING*

By Karen Vercruse

The film *Mississippi Burning* is the true account of one civil-rights struggle in the South in 1964. Three young men who were part of a movement called the Freedom Riders went to Neshoba County, Mississippi, in the summer of 1964 to teach African Americans to read and to register them to vote. The men were brutally murdered by the KKK, which had burned the Mount Zion Methodist Church to the ground, after the three tried to investigate the burning. Amid national outcries for justice, the FBI swept through the county. The federal case for civil-rights violations was prosecuted, and it proved significant to the passage of the national Civil Rights Act of 1964. Although the defendants were found guilty of federal crimes, the state of Mississippi refused to prosecute the murders.

ACTOR GENE HACKMAN (CENTER) ON THE SET OF *MISSISSIPPI BURNING*, A 1988 FILM BASED ON THE 1964 INVESTIGATION OF THE MURDERS OF CHANEY, GOODMAN, AND SCHWERNER, ALSO KNOWN AS THE FREEDOM SUMMER MURDERS, IN PHILADELPHIA, MISSISSIPPI

I was invited to Philadelphia, Mississippi, in 2001, to do research and teach on strategic prayer. As we delved into the spiritual strengths and weaknesses of Neshoba County over the next four years, I realized that many of these intercessors knew little about their own history, or, if they did know, they had not "connected the dots" in spiritual terms. As we inquired of the Lord about strategic prayer, He showed us how to pray "on-site with insight" (to borrow from the title of the book *Prayerwalking,* by Steve Hawthorne and Graham Kendrick). Here are some things that began to come clear:

THE NESHOBA COUNTY COURTHOUSE, IN PHILADELPHIA, MISSISSIPPI

DR. MARTIN LUTHER KING JR. HOLDS A PICTURE OF MICHAEL SCHWERNER, JAMES CHANEY, AND ANDREW GOODMAN, THREE MISSING CIVIL RIGHTS WORKERS KILLED BY THE KU KLUX KLAN WHILE WORKING TO REGISTER BLACK VOTERS DURING THE FREEDOM SUMMER CIVIL RIGHTS CAMPAIGN IN THE SEGREGATED SOUTH. THEIR BRUTAL MURDERS WOULD BECOME A CATALYST FOR THE CIVIL RIGHTS ACT OF 1964

1. There's power in knowing our story. Our history will reveal clues into God's redemptive purposes for our community, as well as strongholds that prevent those purposes. Philadelphia was called to be a "city of brotherly love," but that purpose had been stolen and perverted by the Enemy. Clearly, there was a call for reconciliation and justice coming from the land of Neshoba County, and the blood of innocent victims was crying out for it.

TWO MONTHS AFTER THE CIVIL RIGHTS WORKERS WENT MISSING, THEIR BODIES (LEFT) WERE DISCOVERED UNDER THE THICK, RED CLAY OF AN EARTHEN DAM NEAR PHILADELPHIA. THE BURNED-OUT STATION WAGON THEY WERE DRIVING (RIGHT) WAS FOUND IN A NEARBY SWAMP

2. Come in a spirit opposite to what the Enemy is doing. We began to prayer-walk the County Courthouse in Philadelphia, praying that blessing and justice would replace the iniquity done there. Intercessors built relationships with courthouse workers, asking them for prayer requests and bringing them cards of encouragement. We asked about their current needs, not necessarily those related to city history. We spoke life over locations where there had been death, hope over places where hope had been dashed, and faith over seemingly impossible situations.

3. Pray 'on-site with insight.' We prayed at the site of the murder, the location of the burned-down church, and on the road to the place where the murderers buried the victims.

4. Find, bless, and honor those who have spiritual authority. We met and prayed for an elderly saint who had stood alone against the Klan and had cooperated with the FBI, and she, in turn, prayed for and blessed us. We met and prayed with the new owner/editor of the local paper who proclaimed: "It is my destiny to see justice brought to Neshoba County." We prayed with elected officials and candidates at the annual Neshoba County Fair.

A MEMORIAL AT MT. NEMO MISSIONARY BAPTIST CHURCH HONORS THE MEMORY OF THE THREE CIVIL RIGHTS WORKERS KILLED BY MEMBERS OF THE KU KLUX KLAN, OF THE NESHOBA COUNTY SHERIFF'S OFFICE, AND OF THE PHILADELPHIA POLICE DEPARTMENT IN 1964

(LEFT) BARBARA CHANEY DAILEY, SISTER OF JAMES CHANEY, WATCHES AS RITA SCHWERNER BENDER, WIDOW OF MICHAEL SCHWERNER, LIGHTS A CANDLE AT A MEMORIAL SERVICE TO COMMEMORATE THE 41ST ANNIVERSARY OF THEIR MURDERS. (RIGHT) AFTER THE SERVICE, FORMER FREEDOM RIDERS AND CIVIL RIGHTS ACTIVISTS GATHERED TO HONOR THE VICTIMS

5. Seek reconciliation with those who have been grieved. We met representatives from Mount Zion Church when we attended the annual commemoration service, and we prayed for family members of the three slain Freedom Riders, standing with them for justice.

6. Repent on behalf of those who have committed injustice. Some of the intercessors were related to or had connections with those who had committed the injustice. We identified with their sin, and we asked the Lord and the families of those who were victimized for forgiveness.

KLAN ORGANIZER EDGAR KILLEN (LEFT) WAVES WHILE ENTERING THE COURTROOM IN 1966. KILLEN, A BAPTIST MINISTER, WAS AMONG 18 MEN CHARGED WITH CONSPIRACY IN THE SLAYING OF THREE CIVIL RIGHTS WORKERS (RIGHT). ALTHOUGH ONE OF KILLEN'S FELLOW KLANSMEN IDENTIFIED KILLEN AS THE MAIN INSTIGATOR IN THE KILLINGS, THE JURY WAS DEADLOCKED 11-1. THE LONE HOLDOUT SAID SHE WAS UNABLE TO CONVICT A PREACHER. KILLEN WAS ACQUITTED, AND NO NEW CHARGES WERE BROUGHT BY THE PROSECUTION

7. Persevere. We continued in this process for four years.
In 2004, 40 years after the murders, we saw a breakthrough. The attorney general of Mississippi, Jim Hood, met with a coalition of Philadelphia citizens who were seeking to reopen the murder case.

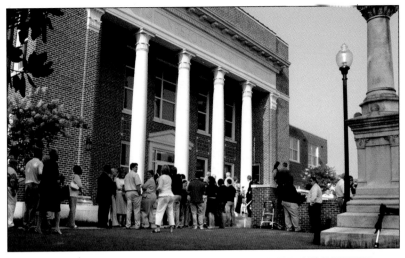

PEOPLE GATHER AT THE NESHOBA COUNTY COURTHOUSE ON THE FINAL DAY OF THE TRIAL

After serious consideration, he agreed. The trial was held at the Neshoba County Courthouse, where we began prayer-walking. We intercessors attended the trial — along with the elderly saint who had bravely stood alone, KKK members who were there to intimidate,

KLANSMAN EDGAR RAY KILLEN IN 1964 (LEFT), AND AT HIS TRIAL IN 2005 (RIGHT). KILLEN WAS FOUND GUILTY ON THREE COUNTS OF MANSLAUGHTER AND ORDERED TO SERVE 60 YEARS IN PRISON. HE DIED IN 2008 AT THE MISSISSIPPI STATE PENITENTIARY

the families of the aggrieved, and the national media. Edgar Ray Killen, an operative for the KKK, was found guilty on June 21, 2005, exactly 41 years to the day the murders had been committed. He had been the pastor of a local church for all those years.

As Jerry Mitchell, a reporter from The (Jackson) Clarion Ledger, later wrote: "What happened in Philadelphia in 2005 continues to serve as an example for this state and this nation as we continue to move toward redemption."

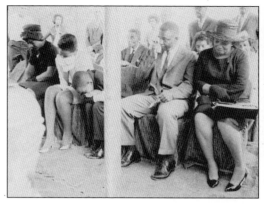 

(LEFT) A YOUNG BEN CHANEY, SEEN HERE WITH HIS FAMILY ON AUG. 7, 1964, WEEPS BY THE CASKET OF HIS OLDER BROTHER, JAMES. (RIGHT) BEN CHANEY 41 YEARS LATER, IN 2005, AFTER THE GUILTY VERDICT WAS ANNOUNCED IN THE KILLING OF HIS BROTHER BY THE KKK

Much has been written about the turn of events surrounding this piece of national history. To be sure, our little band of prayers was only one component of all that the Lord did and of those He used to bring it about. But it is certainly a spiritually significant part of the journey to justice.

ENGAGE:

Have you asked the Lord about the spiritual heritage in your community, both good and evil? Consider joining efforts with others in prayer for your community. Be encouraged by this story that reconciliation and justice are possible even if many decades have passed.

AN ATTENDEE AT SATANCON, IN BOSTON ON APRIL 28, 2023, DURING THE EVENT'S 'SATANIC BALL'

10

GOD'S STRATEGY FOR SATANCON

By Judy McDonough

In 2022, The Satanic Temple (TST) hosted a SatanCon event in Arizona. IFA and many other intercessors stormed heaven (IFA's post about it garnered the most reads in the history of the ministry), and the event fizzled. On-site prayer warriors reported small numbers of attendees and, most thankfully, no chaos.

In 2023, TST planned an event for April 28–30, in Boston. As soon as this was announced, intercessors began praying. The answer was surprising: *Don't pray it out; pray them in.* The Lord spoke clearly to Massachusetts state prayer leaders (and sisters) Suzie and Lynne MacAskill.

Satanists do believe in something: a rebellion against God — usually because they've been deeply wounded by someone in authority over them, or because they've allowed the opening of dangerous doors through poor personal choices or perhaps naivete. God wants intercessors to pray that Christians will see these lost souls as He does;

to look past the costumes, the makeup, and the desperate attempts to repel; and to consider them as deeply valued and loved by God. The Lord wants transformation; He wants hearts that have been changed. Prayer is our most powerful weapon, and we must prepare the fields through prayer. This will be a glorious harvest, but we must have the harvest workers. We can pray for God to send forth the laborers, and He will be faithful to follow through.

SISTERS SUZIE (LEFT) AND LYNNE (RIGHT) MACASKILL, STATE PRAYER LEADERS FOR MASSACHUSETTS

IFA published the strategy the Lord had given, and the response was tremendous. Confirmations of this leading began pouring in. Carol Klussmann had been praying about TST for more than a year. She read about the strategy and immediately contacted IFA. Carol had interceded on-site at the churches in her community since the first SatanCon was reported. *"Here's a plan that has settled in my spirit for me, a person who lives half-of-the-country-away,"* she wrote. *"Those who are spiritually changed as a result of [our prayers] will be at the doors of the church afterwards, returning to locations throughout our country and perhaps the whole world. We need to be ready locally to support their change in allegiance."*

IFA'S PRAYER STRATEGY WENT OUT ACROSS THE NATION

The Church prepared and showed up. Revive Boston had already planned an event for that week. Believers from various organizations and churches joined together in unity. Teams of intercessors prayed on-site, and some even rented the presidential suite of the hotel venue for worship and intercession throughout the conference.

IN THE WEEKS LEADING UP TO THE EVENT, TEAMS OF INTERCESSORS TRAVELED TO BOSTON TO PRAY OVER THE EVENT SITE. THEY SPENT DAYS DISCREETLY WALKING THROUGH THE HOTEL, PRAYING OVER MEETING ROOMS, AND ANOINTING EVERY FLOOR OF THE BUILDING. DURING THE EVENT, OTHER TEAMS OF INTERCESSORS (ABOVE) RENTED ROOMS IN THE HOST HOTEL TO ENGAGE IN ON-SITE PRAYER, WORSHIP AND SPIRITUAL WARFARE

INTERCESSORS BROUGHT SYMBOLIC ITEMS TO THE HOTEL TO HONOR GOD AND REPRESENT THE HISTORY OF GOD'S COVENANT IN MASSACHUSETTS THROUGH THE PILGRIMS OF 1620

There were many opportunities to show kindness and love to those attending, in the name of Jesus. Everyone was peaceful and polite, and we felt God gave us specific prayer assignments, especially on Sunday, that were powerful," Lynne MacAskill said. "You could definitely tell a lot of prayer had gone before us, due to the peaceful nature of the interactions and the openness of many, though definitely not all, of the attendees to dialogue with believers. A lot of them had been raised Christian and had been hurt or oppressed by the Church, so I think that's something we as the Body of Christ need to learn from, so as not to push people away from knowing Jesus. Several evangelists shared with me that although they were opposing the Church, many of them smiled or their eyes softened or even shed tears when they heard the name of Jesus and that He loved them."

SATANCON, HOSTED BY THE SATANIC TEMPLE, FEATURED A 'SATANIC BALL' (ABOVE) AND AN 'UNBAPTISM' CEREMONY HELD IN A 'LITTLE BLACK CHAPEL' (BELOW)

CHRISTIANS KNEEL TO PRAY OUTSIDE THE EVENT VENUE IN BOSTON

As with many prayer realities, the story here is not over. We must persevere in prayer for seeds sown to be watered, cared for, and harvested; for hard soil to be broken up and fertilized in preparation for more seeds to be sown; and for those seeds that have sprouted to grow well and grow strong.

ENGAGE:

Is there something for which you've been praying and where you've seen God answer to a point, but where full restoration has not yet come? God wants you to persevere in prayer; reach out to another believer for partnership in persevering.

A FLAG DECORATES THE FRONT PORCH OF A HOME IN THE HISTORIC FAN DISTRICT OF RICHMOND, VIRGINIA

11

A FIRST FRIDAY MIRACLE

By Gary Bergel

*And seek the peace of the city where I have caused
you to be carried away captive, and pray to the Lord
for it; for in its peace you will have peace
(Jeremiah 29:7 NKJV).*

In the late 1980s, Americans were still experiencing the effects of the 1970s recession, the 1973 oil crisis, and the decline of the global steel market with its gutting of the U.S. steel industry. Globalization had begun, and many U.S. regions saw their manufacturing jobs move overseas. Multitudes of jobless workers found themselves untrained and ill-equipped to find employment in new information-age and service-industry positions. Unemployment, poverty, economic struggles, racial tensions, social decadence, drug addiction and alcoholism, violent crime, and high homicide rates were ravaging entire neighborhoods in many American cities. Consequently, IFA launched an American City Watch in 1986.

Over the course of that year, First Friday Prayer and Fasting was focused specifically on particular U.S. cities. During the 1986 National Day of Prayer observance, all IFA-associated churches were encouraged to intercede for their communities, for neighboring towns and cities, and for the state on the whole. A general awakening to the histories; migration patterns; racial and cultural conflicts; crises; and other urgent conditions in America's population centers began spreading across the nation.

Pastors and believers from a wide range of church backgrounds began to network and to study the spiritual and social histories of their own communities. Dedicated teams prayerfully documented both the negative and positive influences in the formation of their regions. They investigated how Native American shamanism, Colonial American Freemasonry, slavery, wars, racial conflicts, injustice, prejudice, political divisiveness, crime, and other forms of spiritual and social corruption became enthroned — established as strongholds through which demonic forces could inflict spiritual wounds and promote oppression and discord over entire generations.

These research teams also documented unique giftings and positive contributions from Native American peoples; from pioneers and settlers; and from church, civic, and business leaders. They drilled into times of revival and divine visitation, and they rediscovered some long-lost prophetic utterances.

Richmond, Virginia, which had been the Civil War Confederate capital, became one of the seedbeds for these discoveries and teachings. A citywide prayer movement began to form, uniting pastors and believers across the city and the region. A multiethnic assembly, spearheaded by pastors Douglas McMurry and Wellington Boone, began to meet

THE STATE CAPITAL OF RICHMOND SURROUNDED BY RUINS AFTER THE EVACUATION FIRE OF 1865, WHEN THE CONFEDERATE ARMY ATTEMPTED TO BURN THE CITY DOWN DURING THE CIVIL WAR

monthly. Leading pastors and intercessors repented for the initiation of slave trading in Virginia by Richmond's founder, William Byrd II; for related injustices; for broken treaties with and the unjust treatment of the Native American tribes; and for the vice and corruption that resulted from the tobacco and liquor trades. Many historical root matters came to be addressed in intercessory prayer.

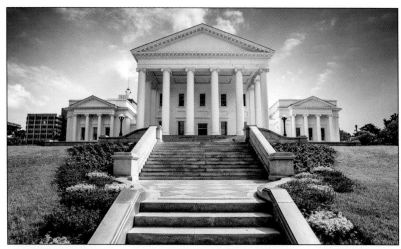

A MODERN VIEW OF THE STATE CAPITOL BUILDING FEATURES THE 1904 ADDITION OF WINGS ON EACH SIDE TO PROVIDE SPACE FOR THE GROWING VIRGINIA LEGISLATURE

In a real and continuing way, spiritual elders were restored in the gates of the city of Richmond. They began to bind and loose. This sort of restoration of reconciled relationships and prayerful fellowship in Christ pleases God and invites His manifest presence.

During one First Friday weekend assembly, God showed up and surprised the city and the "Church at Richmond," as many leaders and believers had begun to see and call themselves. In his book, *The Church at Richmond*, McMurry documented how God went beyond words and bound the strongman of murder (see Matthew 12:29).

Boone and Pastor Louis Skidmore invited Gary Bergel, IFA's president, to lead an intercessors' conference. More than 700 intercessors packed St. Giles Presbyterian Church on Feb. 9–11.

The intercession focused on Richmond's murder rate — the second-highest per capita in the nation.

THE CITY SKYLINE OF RICHMOND, VIRGINIA, AT DUSK

For the next month, no murders occurred in Richmond, starting on Feb. 9! Police Lt. W.E. Harver said: "Whatever forces are at work to keep the murders down, I hope they keep working."

McMurry wrote: "The Church at Richmond had managed to produce a unified voice in prayer, led by pastors who were determined to see Richmond transformed out of its reputation as a murder capital in the nation. God had responded by cutting off murders, as a clear sign of His desire to answer the prayers of the saints."

ENGAGE:

Seek God's intervention to prevent murders and other violent crimes on our streets. Pray specifically for your own city, and bring others in to pray with you.

12

COMPLAINING DOESN'T BRING CHANGE – *PRAYER* DOES

By Nicole Arnoldbik

Christians in Chico, California, had had enough. *Playboy* magazine ranked California State University, Chico, the No. 2 party school in the nation in 2001 (it was No. 1 in 1987). A Mardi Gras atmosphere characterized the city, and its reputation for drinking and lawlessness grew as the annual Pioneer Days festival led to out-of-control (often violent) Halloween celebrations. Nearly 25,000 people descended on Chico every year in October, making the residents feel like strangers in their own neighborhoods — not to mention powerless and even complicit.

"By and large, people stay away from downtown and complain about it," said Larry Lane, a pastor who had been involved in city outreach efforts in the Chico area since 1992. "Believers followed suit. I complained too, but the Lord spoke to my heart in 1999 and said it was a problem for the Church to do something about, not a problem of the city."

KENDALL HALL ADMINISTRATION BUILDING, AT CHICO STATE

For several years, nine pastors had been meeting together for weekly prayer. Pastor Lane told the group he felt moved to do something about Chico's darkness. He had watched The Sentinel Group's Transformations video, highlighting communities globally that had been changed through the prayers and repentance of local Christians, and he thought, "Why not Chico?" Instead of a kids-will-be-kids mentality, why couldn't the churches raise the bar for this university town by adopting a zero-tolerance (kids-will-be-transformed) mentality and chasing the darkness away with light?

THE SENATOR THEATRE, IN DOWNTOWN CHICO

Pastor Lane and others researched Chico's history, meditated on Scripture, and outlined a strategy. They recognized the celebrations as a form of false worship rooted in paganism, and they asked, "What would happen if true worship took place simultaneously?" They secured the downtown gazebo in the park and scheduled various churches to plan a time of praise and worship.

CHICO CITY PLAZA, A POPULAR SITE FOR OUTDOOR GATHERINGS IN DOWNTOWN CHICO

On the night of the event, everyone was nervous, including the police! The tension grew, and the volunteer intercessors and worshipers began to second-guess their plans.

"People stood shoulder-to-shoulder, and fights broke out in the crowd," said Pastor Lane. "Many were drinking to excess. The police asked us to go. If you can picture a crowd dressed in Halloween outfits and risqué costumes, and a typical Sunday morning worship team leading worship in the middle of this, that's what it looked like."

But when the Holy Spirit descended and the presence of the Lord entered the park, some of those who had been mocking the worship team became silent. Three girls in Playboy bunny costumes had been dancing sensually but then stopped and began to cry. Others were in tears also.

That night, 13 people gave their lives to Christ. Prodigals felt the presence of the Lord as He penetrated the darkness and made Himself known through the worship. Intercessors' faith was strengthened as they saw what God could do through obedience and a willingness to match faith with action.

THE CAMPUS OF CALIFORNIA STATE UNIVERSITY, CHICO

Chico's transformation is still unfolding. Intercessors give testimony that God is defying reliance upon a formula by forcing them to humbly rely on the Holy Spirit for each next step. There is no cookie-cutter program.

"As we prayed in year two, God spoke to us to stay out of downtown [during the Halloween celebration] and pray within our churches

THE TRINITY BELL TOWER, ON THE CAMPUS OF CHICO STATE

around the city," said Pastor Lane. Surprisingly, year two was a nightmare. A stabbing occurred, and people inquired of their leaders why the prayers had failed to change things.

Yet, God knew what He was doing. One of the hallmarks of the prayer journey has been the relationships between key city leaders and the Body of Christ. That January, after intercessors wrestled for several months seeking clarity, the Council experienced a "shift." Officials voted to shut down the event completely and asked the police department to help. By the third year, they had put an end to the event. In addition, Chico's police chief received Christ.

"I told the police department: 'You need to know there's an umbrella of prayer over this city, like a geodesic dome, and tonight is going to be a night of peace,' " said Pastor Lane, recalling the domino effect of blessing. A light has dawned and continues to rise as faithful intercessors seek the Lord to transform the darkness (see Isaiah 9:2).

ENGAGE:

Are there any public events in your city that generate a negative, destructive environment? How might you reach out to civic, business, and church leaders to seek solutions? Pray for God's leading, guidance, and help.

13

FROM 'DEPRESSED CITY USA' TO CITY OF HOPE

By Arlyn Lawrence

"You're from Clay County? Ohhh ... "

A knowing comment and a condescending lift of the eyebrows were typical responses whenever someone admitted to being a resident of what was once the second-poorest county in Kentucky and the fourth-poorest in the nation. In 1964, CBS News gave the small city of Manchester — Clay County's county seat — the title of "Depressed City, USA." Forty years later, in 2004, nothing had changed; if anything, the situation was worse.

The community was divided — not just physically, by geography, but also relationally, from years of violent clan feuding. The churches were divided — marked by spiritual pride and parochial bickering that left them stripped of any real spiritual power or meaningful role in the public arena. Families were divided — destroyed by divorce, rampant drug and alcohol abuse, abandonment, and suicide. There was widespread crime too. There were more people incarcerated in the local prison than residing in the town. Even law enforcement was divided and impotent, riddled with corruption and devoid of any cooperation among the various agencies. From all the visible signs, the scenario for Manchester, Kentucky, was increasingly hopeless.

A Desperate Place

Out of sheer desperation, Christians began to pray together. About 100 to 150 of them started gathering on Saturday mornings — fed up with the loss of far too many bright young lives due to drug overdoses. They were also fed up with the corruption and the crime — fed up with drug dealers whose houses got more commercial traffic than the local Wendy's, while law officials turned a blind eye. One participant put it

simply: "People just got tired of burying their kids." So, they gathered, from all walks of life, praying across denominational lines: Presbyterians, Methodists, Baptists, charismatics, and Catholics. Even those who were not professing Christians showed up to pray, so great was their desperation. One pastor reported: "People who had never done that before were on their knees crying out to God, and all of a sudden you're hugging a Presbyterian or a Methodist." Instead of focusing on their differences, they were now focusing on their commonalities: *Jesus and their community's problems.*

Repenting, and Exposing the Darkness

What did those desperate, united prayers look like? For one, participants repented (as churches and as individuals) for their passivity, disunity, and spiritual separatism that had robbed the Church of its rightful role and responsibility in the community. "We weren't

[just] trying to take back what the devil had stolen," said Pastor Doug Abner of Community Church, in Manchester. "We were taking back what was rightfully ours that we had given up because the Church wasn't doing what it was supposed to have done." One Methodist minister said at the beginning of the prayer meetings: "We need to pray for God to expose the darkness." So they did. And God responded.

Little did the praying band of believers know that God was already moving powerfully behind the scenes to break open the crime and corruption that had poisoned the community for so long. Unbeknownst to anyone, the FBI had quietly moved into town and was working intensely behind the scenes.

It is notable that those Saturday morning prayer gatherings were not the first foray into seeking spiritual solutions to the community's practical difficulties. On Sept. 7, 2002, a historic prayer initiative took place at the Cumberland Gap, just 40 miles southeast of Manchester. That gathering brought several thousand intercessors from some 40 states

A VIEW OF THE CUMBERLAND GAP, WHICH BORDERS VIRGINIA, TENNESSEE, AND KENTUCKY

and included representatives from Scotland, Ireland, and Wales — from which originated the settlers who traversed the Gap in the earliest years of America's history. The intercessors believed fervently that God would pour out His Spirit through the Gap, just as hundreds of thousands of pioneers had poured through it centuries earlier. That day, ten cities in the Kentucky region banded together to form a prayer corridor in preparation for revival in the region, and they prayed words of healing over the land.

Taking a Stand and Welcoming Jesus

Two years later, those prayers came to powerful fruition on May 2, 2004, as 63 churches and roughly 3,500 people came together on a cold, rainy day to march in the streets against drugs in Manchester. "ENOUGH!" roared the newspaper headlines the next day, for that was the battle cry, both practically and spiritually. John Becknell, president of CCMP-TV, in Manchester, says the people knew the march that day wasn't just about taking a stand against drugs; it was about welcoming Jesus as Lord of Clay County and consciously re-enthroning Him as the ruler over the land and people. Alongside the anti-drug banners, marchers lifted high signs reading: "Lord of Lords" and "Jesus is Lord in Clay County."

Many people in Manchester will tell of their conviction that this climactic prayer event broke the vice-like grip of drug addiction and other issues that had

tormented the daily life of the entire region. Within roughly two months, the FBI closed in and made its move. Subsequently, over the next several years, more than 3,000 people were arrested, including drug dealers. Seventy county officials were indicted. The mayor, the city supervisor, Council members, commissioners, the assistant police chief, the fire chief, county clerks, and even a circuit judge presiding over three counties were exposed and jailed for racketeering, distributing drugs, and voter fraud. Corrupt members of the police and sheriff's departments were exposed, prosecuted, and sent to prison. New, stable, and accountable government was installed, which has had far-reaching effects.

True Transformation

In fact, residents of Manchester will be the first to tell you that there has been a distinct "before" and "after" in the community — before the prayer started, before the march, and after. And that before-and-after effect can best be described as transformation:

- Crime and corruption have diminished dramatically throughout the community.
- Economic conditions have improved, leading to a discernible lessening of poverty.
- New laws, school curricula, and business practices have been put into effect.
- Political leaders have publicly acknowledged their previous sin and their renewed dependence on God.
- Restored hope and joy have led to marked declines in divorce, bankruptcy, and suicide.

- Secular media and government have confirmed growing social and political renewal.
- Volunteerism has increased as Christians have recognized their responsibility to care for their community.
- Large numbers of local drug dealers and addicts have surrendered their lives to Jesus Christ and been dramatically delivered from drug addiction.

In 2007, the City Council voted to change the name of the city to Manchester — City of Hope. The city has become a regional influence, receiving desperate calls from 49 states and five foreign nations, all soliciting guidance in their own battles against drugs.

George Otis Jr., founder and president of The Sentinel Group, documented the transformation of Manchester, Kentucky, in the documentary *An Appalachian Dawn*. After thousands of hours of research, interviews, filming, editing, and the resulting video production of the dramatic and moving story, Otis says much of the story remains untold. "It was the hardest story for us to tell," he recounts, "because, where do I start? What is the best angle? There are so many possibilities. I can't even begin to overstate what God has done here." After having observed and/or documented transformational revivals in some 700 communities around the world, Otis agrees that Manchester, Kentucky, is a classic example — and all the more exciting because it is in America. It's an example of what happens, he says, when people take seriously what God promises in Scripture: *"... if my people who are called by my name will humble themselves and pray and seek my face and turn from their wicked ways, I will hear from heaven and will forgive their sins and restore their land"* (2 Chronicles 7:14 NLT).

That's exactly what happened in Manchester: confession; repentance; humbling; action. "People in this story who, from a theological perspective, are oil and water, are joined at the hip in what God is doing," said Otis. "That's a hallmark of genuine revival."

Returning to Repentance, Prayer, and Unity

In 2011, seven years after the original prayer meetings and the march, they were getting back to repentance, reports Otis. As with all movements of God, there can be a tendency to rest on one's laurels (or one's blessings) and take for granted what God has done. The key, Otis says, is to stay in humility, stay in dependence on the Lord, and stay in prayer. Church and civic leaders alike in Manchester took seriously the responsibility to stay in  prayer and unity. Because of this, God's presence and work were still keenly felt and observed in the public arena in Manchester.

"We don't always see right away everything that God is doing in response to our prayers," Otis said. "Sometimes, He's moving behind the scenes in response to our prayers in ways we can't even see — yet. When He does manifest His presence, you'll always know it, not just by the nature of His response, but by its magnitude and force."

A MIST RISES OVER THE ROLLING HILLS OF KENTUCKY

Attracting God's Attention

But though God's response to our prayers may vary from community to community, the thing that remains constant is what He tells us will attract His attention and His presence. These are the very things the Manchester churches set into motion, whether or not they realized it at the time. They understood that the problems were spiritual, not just physical. They united in desperation and repentance. They began to pray for a solution. And they started taking action. The resulting transformation is beyond the scope of most people's ability to describe. Perhaps Becknell's simple assessment says it best. He just tells people: "God tabernacled here."

As many of the people in the Manchester story will testify, when we humble ourselves before the Lord and repent individually, we have the platform to come together to repent and pray corporately. When we do this, we cultivate a spiritual appetite and atmosphere in which the Lord can do amazing things among us.

ENGAGE:

"Consecrate yourselves," Joshua told the Israelites, "for tomorrow the Lord will do amazing things among you" (Joshua 3:5). Consecrate means "to purify." We purify ourselves through humility, confession of sin, and repentance. God wanted to do something wonderful for the community as a whole. But first He asked them to purify themselves individually. This meant careful self-examination, humility, honest confession, and earnest repentance of any revealed sin. Take time to consecrate yourself, and see what God will do.

A VIEW OF THE CAPITOL BUILDING IN WASHINGTON D.C. AT SUNRISE

14

D.C. CRIME RATE PLUMMETS

By IFA Staff

In January of 1990, IFA joined Together In Ministry (TIM) to spearhead a 90-hour prayer-and-fasting vigil during the first week of the year in the District of Columbia. Multiethnic assemblies met each evening at historic churches. Much intercessory work concerning the city was done, leading to a "breakthrough" jubilee time at the close of the vigil. In mid-January, an intercessory prayer conference was convened at New Covenant Fellowship, in nearby Northern Virginia. The Lord assigned the group to bind "deception" in Washington. It was on that very night that then-Mayor Marion Barry was caught in the act of smoking crack cocaine and arrested. That day began a purging of corruption and a renewal of "good government" in our nation's capital.

Dan Wedderburn, of the D.C. Human Rights Commission, wrote this in a Washington Post letter to the editor in May 2000:

Most people know that crime in New York City has declined dramatically in recent years. But how many know that crime in Washington has fallen just as dramatically?

THE WASHINGTON MONUMENT, COMPLETED IN 1884 TO MEMORIALIZE PRESIDENT GEORGE WASHINGTON, PIERCES THE SKYLINE OF THE NATIONAL MALL IN WASHINGTON, D.C.

Crime in the District of Columbia fell 32 percent from 1993 to 1998, and in 1999 it dropped an additional 14 percent, according to preliminary police figures. Thus, crime in the district has been nearly halved in the past six years.

Of more significance, violent crime – murder, rape, robbery and aggravated assault – is down 60 percent. Remember D.C.'s nickname of "murder capital?" Well, the number of murders in the city dropped from 454 in 1993 to 232 last year. Rape in the District has fallen more than 40 percent, while aggravated assault and robberies are both down about 60 percent and burglaries by 70 percent.

The District's precipitous drop in crime far exceeds the national average. Across the country, crime fell 12 percent from 1993 to 1998, while crime in Washington dropped 32 percent. The city's reduced crime rate also compares favorably with crime-rate reduction in its suburbs of Montgomery, Prince George's and Fairfax counties, where, during the same period of 1993 to 1998, crime fell 4 percent, 5 percent and 7 percent, respectively. ...

What accounts for the significant reduction in crime in recent years? The reasons are unclear but appear to include the robust economy, low unemployment, fewer people in younger-age categories that account for a disproportionate share of crime, record high incarcerations and better policing strategies.

TRAFFIC ON PENNSYLVANIA AVENUE IN FRONT OF THE CAPITOL BUILDING ILLUMINATED AT NIGHT

Other factors contributing to the District's reduced crime are the significant decline in crack-cocaine trafficking and open-air drug markets, and the demolition of more than 1,500 units of public housing, the site of much violent crime. Of special note in the mix is the fact that the number of D.C. police officers declined 20 percent during the city's dramatic reduction in crime, from 4,372 officers in 1993 to 3,488 at the end of October 1999. ...

THE JEFFERSON MEMORIAL AND WASHINGTON MONUMENT REFLECT ON THE TIDAL BASIN AT NIGHT IN WASHINGTON, D.C.

IFA began a monthly Washington Watch prayer effort in late 1992, just months before the noted drop in crime began. More than 5,000 intercessors subscribed to the alerts, which included prayer points related to D.C. officials, crime, and the police department.

A group of national leaders initiated a nationwide, 24-hour U.S./D.C. Prayer Watch in 1997, with at least one person interceding all the time for the nation's capital; the top 120 civic officials; ambassadors and nations represented by embassies; pastors and church leaders; specific neighborhoods; and all of the city's residents — and pages of the phone directory were mailed to everyone who signed up to pray. Several Christian members of Congress held weekly prayer meetings for D.C., and city leaders and pastors often participated.

Scores of local congregations and various ministries held weekly prayer meetings for the city too. A 24-hour Capital Region Revival Prayer Watch offered year-round prayer in local churches. Though Wedderburn wrote that the reasons for the historic drop in crime were unclear, it is likely that these concerted, united, persistent prayer efforts for Washington were among those reasons.

ENGAGE:

Set aside dedicated prayer time to intercede specifically for the crime rate in our nation's capital and in your area, and reach out to other intercessors who will join you in those prayers.

You did not choose me, but I chose you and appointed you that you should go and bear fruit and that your fruit should abide, so that whatever you ask the Father in my name, he may give it to you (John 15:16).

For we are his workmanship, created in Christ Jesus for good works, which God prepared beforehand, that we should walk in them (Ephesians 2:10).

If a brother or sister is poorly clothed and lacking in daily food, and one of you says to them, "Go in peace, be warmed and filled," without giving them the things needed for the body, what good is that? So also faith by itself, if it does not have works, is dead (James 2:15–17).

PART 3:
ADDING ACTION TO INTERCESSION

———◆———

There are times we pray for someone or something, and that is all the Lord asks of us. But there are other times in which the Lord asks us to be the answer to our own prayers and to take actions inspired by those prayers. This is a gift from Him, because then we get to see Him work in specific and miraculous ways. Prayer and action are required of us.

15

PRAYER AND THE BELTWAY SNIPERS

By Ron Lantz

Traffic on I-70 wasn't too bad. I should have been enjoying myself that day in October, sitting up in the cab of my 18-wheeler, cruising through the Pennsylvania hills.

Thirty-six years as a trucker, and I still get a kick out of my rig. Bass Transportation bought this 600-horsepower tractor in 2000. I was the only one who drove it, and although I logged almost 400,000 miles, the cab was still so clean you could eat off the floor. If traffic held steady, I would make my usual run right on schedule, hauling a tanker of building compound from Ohio to Delaware, then deadheading back to my home in Ludlow, Kentucky.

But I didn't make the run on time that day, and for the same reason I wasn't enjoying the trip: the Beltway sniper. The words hammered in my head. Eight dead and two wounded already and it didn't look like there'd be an end to it. At any truck stop in the D.C. area, all we talked about was the white van the police were looking for. Schools were closed, people too scared to leave their homes. It weighed on me that this guy was out there getting ready to kill again. I knew what it was like to lose someone you love. Five years earlier my wife, Ruth, and I lost our only son, Ron, to multiple sclerosis.

It was a pretty October day just like this one when he died. I knew when I got to the nursing home that something was up, because there was a lot of hollering down the hall. "What's going on?" I asked.

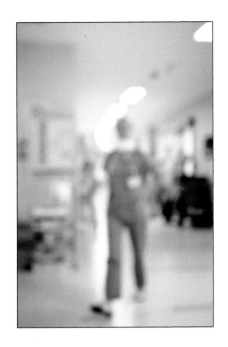

"It's your son, Mr. Lantz," a nurse said.

I hurried to Ron's room. There was our boy sitting on the edge of his bed, hands raised over his head, praising the Lord. For more than a year he hadn't been able to sit up on his own.

"I'm leaving here," Ron said. "Someone's coming through that door tonight to take me home." Then he looked at me really hard. "Dad, I don't want to be up in heaven waiting for you and you don't make it."

It wasn't the first time he'd brought up the subject. Ron was a real committed Christian. My parents raised me in the faith, but somehow I'd drifted away. "I want you to go over to my church right now," Ron went on. "Find my pastor and give your life to the Lord."

Well, that's exactly what I did. Afterward I went back to the nursing home and told Ron. I'm glad I had the chance, because Somebody did come for my boy that night and took him home.

My life turned around. I got active in church. I headed the men's fellowship, led retreats, was on the Sunday school board. I'd never start a run without kneeling by my bed at the rear of the cab and asking God to watch over Ruth.

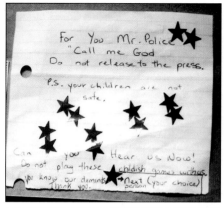

A NOTE FOUND NEAR THE SCENE OF ONE OF THE SNIPER SHOOTINGS, IN ASPEN HILL, MARYLAND

After the sniper shot his first victims, I'd been praying about that, too — that someone would stop this killing spree. It had gone on for 12 days already. Around 7 p.m., when I was about an hour and a half out of Wilmington, Delaware, the usual report came on the radio. Nothing new on the sniper. All they knew was that a white van might be involved.

I got to thinking about what I'd learned at church, how a bunch of people praying together can be more powerful than a person praying alone. What if I get on my CB, to see if a few drivers want to pull off the road with me and pray about this?

I pressed the button on my microphone and said that if anyone wanted to pray about the sniper, he could meet me in half an hour at the eastbound 66-mile-marker rest area. A trucker answered right away. Then another and another. They'd be there. I hadn't gone 5 miles before a line of trucks formed, some coming up from behind, others up ahead slowing down to join us. The line stretched for miles.

It was getting dark when we pulled into the rest area. There must have been 50 rigs there. We all got out of our cabs and stood in a circle, holding hands, 60 or 70 of us, including some wives and children.

"Let's pray," I said. "Anyone who feels like it can start." Well, the first one to speak up was a kid maybe 10 years old, standing just to my left. The boy bowed his head: "Our Father, who art in heaven…"

We went around the circle, some folks using their own words, others using phrases from the Lord's Prayer. It seemed to me there was a special meaning where it says, " … *deliver us from evil.* … "

A POLICE VIDEO DEMONSTRATES HOW THE SNIPERS TARGETED VICTIMS FROM THE TRUNK OF THEIR CAR

The last person finished praying. We had prayed for 59 minutes. All those truckers adding an hour to their busy schedules!

Ten days later, on Oct. 23, I was making my Ohio to Delaware run again. There had been another killing, and the sniper was no nearer to being caught.

Right from the start there was something a bit different about my trip. In the first place, it was a Wednesday. I normally made my runs on Tuesdays and Thursdays. But there was a delay at the loading dock, so I told my pastor I'd have to miss our Wednesday night prayer meeting. "We'll be praying for you," he said.

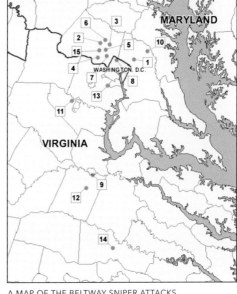

A MAP OF THE BELTWAY SNIPER ATTACKS

The second thing: I was stopped by cops. Once was rare for me; this trip I was pulled over three times. Not for very long, they were just checking papers, but it made me late getting into Wilmington.

The next strange thing: Instead of catching a few hours of sleep, I headed back west as soon as my cargo was offloaded at around 11 p.m. That wasn't like me at all. It was like I had an appointment, like I couldn't sleep even if I tried.

FBI AGENTS INVESTIGATE THE SCENE OF A SNIPER ATTACK IN THE WASHINGTON, D.C. AREA

At midnight *The Truckin' Bozo* show came on the air, a music and call-in program a lot of truckers listen to. There was news in the sniper case. There were two snipers, not one, and police now believed the guys were driving a blue 1990 Chevrolet Caprice with New Jersey plates, license number NDA-21Z.

I wrote down the tag number. Just before 1 a.m., I reached the rest stop at the 39-mile marker near Myersville, Maryland, only a few miles from where so many of us had made a circle and prayed.

And here was the last weird thing about that trip. The truck aisles were full. I'd never seen so many rigs at that stop, drivers asleep. The only thing I could do was swing around to the car section. I wouldn't be long. Climbing down from my cab, I noticed a car in the No Parking Zone. The light over the men's room door was shining right on it.

A blue Chevrolet Caprice. There must be hundreds of blue Caprices out there. I looked closer; two men, one slumped over the wheel, asleep. Beyond the men's room was a row of bushes. I crept behind them and squinted to make out the license number. Jersey plates. N … DA2 … 1 … Z.

THE LICENSE PLATE OF THE BLUE CHEVROLET CAPRICE FIRST SPOTTED BY LANTZ (LEFT), AND THE SAME CAR AFTER IT WAS RECOVERED BY POLICE

Quiet as I could, I climbed back in my rig. Better not use the CB, in case those guys have one. I punched 911 on my cell phone. "I'm at the Myersville rest stop. There's a blue Chevrolet Caprice here, Jersey license NDA-21Z."

The operator asked me to hold on. In a minute she came back with instructions. Wait there. Don't let them see you. Block the exit with your truck if you can.

If an 18-wheeler can tiptoe, that's what mine did. I blocked as much of the exit ramp as I could, but there was still room for a car to get by. Five minutes passed. Only one other driver was ready to roll. Soon as I told him what was happening, he pulled his rig alongside mine, sealing off the exit. I sat in my cab, looking out the side mirrors at that blue Caprice, expecting a shootout, thinking I ought to be scared and wondering why I wasn't.

Five more minutes passed. I was afraid another truck or a car would drive up and honk for us to move it, waking the suspects, but no one stirred. The cops slid up so quiet I didn't know they were there until suddenly it was the Fourth of July with flash-grenades lighting up the night to stun the two men. Next thing I knew the two men were being led away.

Since I'd been blocking the exit, I was the first one out. Five miles down the road I started shaking so badly I could hardly hold the wheel. Then I got to thinking about all the unusual things that had to happen for me to be at that place at that time and about my friends at church praying for me that same evening. And I couldn't help thinking about my son, Ron, who'd led me to that church.

RON LANTZ WITH REPORTERS AFTER THE BELTWAY SNIPERS WERE APPREHENDED

I looked in my rearview mirror at the line of trucks behind me and remembered leading another line of semis 10 days earlier. I remembered the circle of truckers and their families, holding hands, voices joined together to pray *"... deliver us from evil."*

JOHN ALLEN MUHAMMAD (LEFT), AND HIS ACCOMPLICE LEE BOYD MALVO (RIGHT), WERE BOTH CONVICTED OF MURDERING TEN PEOPLE DURING THE 2002 D.C. SNIPER ATTACKS

A SOLD-OUT NEWSPAPER RACK IN D.C. ANNOUNCES THE CAPTURE OF THE BELTWAY SNIPERS

ENGAGE:

Do you believe that "a bunch of people praying together can be more powerful than a person praying alone," and that the Father is willing to do for them what they ask? Consider how you might gather together with others in Christ's name as "two or three" to agree on earth about anything.

16

PARENTS AND A SCHOOL REVOLUTION

By Judy McDonough

When schools shut down for COVID in the early spring of 2020, children began attending school virtually, from their homes, with their parents close by. Insiders and intercessors who had prayed about and watched education in America knew that unbiblical and incorrect ideas were regularly taught in the nation's public schools. But it had been a hard sell to awaken parents and citizens to recognize this, to care, and to take action.

In April 2020, IFA asked intercessors to pray very specifically about the content of the curriculum being used in schools. Here's what writer and education expert Nancy Huff wrote:

"In the wake of COVID, public schools are issuing electronic devices to hundreds of thousands of students for curriculum delivery. Parents who may have never cracked one of their children's public school textbooks, now have a golden opportunity to truly discover what's in all those books their children have been packing around for years. Parents are now able to read textbooks, watch classroom videos, and sit in on a teacher presenting a lesson. At this time, parents have an excellent opportunity to become involved with what their children learn, and at the same time, develop a prayer strategy for those in the textbook industry responsible for lessons presented in the classroom."

The article addressed how new social ideas had been woven into even elementary school textbooks. At the time, hardly anyone had heard of critical race theory (CRT). Huff explained how history was being framed and retold, and she made this important point: "We put a tremendous burden on our students when they are made to feel guilty for historical events over which they had no say or control. We are opening a sore that can never heal, with a curriculum based on blame." Now we see that Huff was absolutely right.

Huff urged Christian parents to keep informed and to take action: "For the Christian parent, the discovery of questionable content presented in the classroom can be shocking.

LOUDOUN COUNTY, VIRGINIA, PARENTS PRAY AFTER BEING EXPELLED FROM A SCHOOL BOARD MEETING FOR CLAPPING IN AGREEMENT WITH A SPEAKER

Many will have their suspicions verified that there is an 'education cartel' in this country aimed at furthering a social and political agenda rather than the promotion of literacy, historical facts, and scientific knowledge. Parents, with greater ease than ever before, can investigate the educational content presented to their children. Parents who

EDUCATION EXPERT AND IFA WRITER NANCY HUFF, SPEAKING AT THE UNITED NATIONS

recognize the spiritual battle in which we are engaged will pray, not to demolish publishing companies, but rather attack the spiritual structures in which those businesses trust. Now is an excellent time to develop prayer strategies that establish godly principles and accurate knowledge in the school curriculum."

Years of being a faithful watchman in education had positioned Huff to call the nation's intercessors to pray for parents, while COVID gave them a front-row seat to what she had seen happening for years.

PARENTS PROTEST BEFORE A SCHOOL BOARD MEETING IN TAMPA, FLORIDA

A PARENT SPEAKS DURING A PUBLIC FORUM AT THE HILLSBOROUGH COUNTY SCHOOL BOARD MEETING IN TAMPA, FLORIDA

The answer to these prayers astounded almost everyone in America. Parents "woke" up to the woke agenda in the schools, and they moved into action. School board meetings started making headlines as parents challenged CRT — from kindergarten through high school. Not only revisionist history, but also pornographic materials deceptively described as "sex education" were discovered in libraries and classrooms across the nation.

Parents prayed, spoke out, filed lawsuits, and ran for school board election. Christian teachers boldly refused to call biological boys "girls" — risking their jobs in the process and facing harassment and even death threats.

God used COVID to expose things hidden from the light, and He inspired us to pray that things would change. And things are changing.

A FAMILY CARRIES U.S. FLAGS AND PROTEST SIGNS DURING THE KENTUCKY FREEDOM RALLY AT THE CAPITOL BUILDING IN FRANKFORT, KENTUCKY

ENGAGE:

Keep praying for American schools. Pray for every kind of school. As you pray, confess that the Almighty owns the schools, the school system, the nation, and every family.

ABORTION
stops *a beating heart*

17

MARK LEE DICKSON: SANCTUARY CITIES FOR THE UNBORN

By Suni Piper

Mark Lee Dickson, pastor of Sovereign Love Church, was already director of Right to Life of East Texas when his associate pastor invited him to come stand on the sidewalks outside a local abortion clinic. Pastor Mark went begrudgingly. He was quickly offended by the loud voices of those out there preaching and fighting for life. For his part, he never wanted to be a street preacher, being content to confine his own preaching to listeners in the pews. But his discomfort that day caused him to check himself and ask God why all the pro-life sidewalk preaching rubbed him the wrong way. *Is there anything wrong with what the street preacher is saying?* thought Mark restlessly. *Is there anything wrong with how he's saying it? Or is it just different to me, and I'm just not used to this?*

Mark did believe in the power of public preaching, being drawn to the likes of George Whitfield and John Wesley. But as for doing *himself* anything like what they had done, he felt a battle raging internally. Ultimately, he sensed the Lord ask him: "Is Church history your standard, or is the word of God your standard?"

DICKSON HOLDS UP A NEWSPAPER BEARING A HISTORIC HEADLINE IN FRONT OF THE SUPREME COURT BUILDING, IN WASHINGTON, D.C.

Today Mark stands on those very same sidewalks boldly sharing the gospel, the hope of new life in Christ and the help of those who choose that life. He regularly hears from the mothers: "I was going to kill my child, but you were there, and God sent you there to save my life!"

"Abortion facilities are not fun places to be at," he said. "But abortion facilities are places we need to be as a presence on that sidewalk, praying and sharing the word of God with anyone who will listen as we offer true hope and encouragement to men and women who are about to make a horrible decision, with hopes that we might convince them to not go forward with that decision."

When Mark heard from one of these mothers that there were plans to shut down the abortion facility, he felt *concern* in his heart, rather than any immediate sense of jubilee. As the details unfolded, he recalled that in the early 1990s, the director of that same facility had said someone in the Houston area pledged land and a building for an abortion clinic in Waskom, Texas.

In May 2019, Mark shared his concern about that potential abortion clinic with the mayor of Waskom. When the mayor asked what he could do, Mark replied: "Pass an ordinance outlawing abortion within the city limits."

A few weeks later, Waskom became the first sanctuary city for the unborn. Dozens of communities have followed, not only in Texas, but also in Illinois, Iowa, Louisiana, Missouri, Nebraska, New Mexico, and Ohio.

Mark asserts that no matter how big or small a city might be, its people can take a stand, and America can be transformed to support life — zip code by zip code. "If your elected officials will not do what is moral and right, then find people who will do what is moral and right, get them to run for office, and vote those who will not do what is moral and right out," he said. "Get people into office that are going to care more about what God wants for the city."

ENGAGE:

Begin praying that life would prevail within your own zip code. When praying with others, lift up their zip codes too, asking God to make them into sanctuaries of life.

THE GATE AT DACHAU CONCENTRATION CAMP READS: 'WORK SETS YOU FREE'

18

RESCUING THE PERISHING

By Gloria Robles

K im Primavera is a wife, a mother of six, a writer, an intercessor, and chairwoman of the village of Hayes Center, Nebraska, now a "sanctuary city" for the unborn. In high school, Primavera visited Germany on a school trip. At the Dachau Concentration Camp, she was thinking: *Why didn't anyone do something? How could millions die so easily?* She has felt that same way about abortion, asking herself: *Why is it socially acceptable? Why are millions of babies dying?* This led her to take action. Primavera started "life chains," organized prayer meetings, and joined the board of trustees in her city.

Pastor Mark Lee Dickson's fight to establish sanctuary cities for the unborn in Texas, as featured by IFA, moved Primavera deeply. After seeing what was accomplished in Carbon, Texas, she asked: "Why can't we do this in Hayes Center, Nebraska?"

MARK LEE DICKSON (STANDING, LEFT) MEETS WITH KIM PRIMAVERA (SEATED, FAR RIGHT) AND OTHER TOWN OFFICIALS FROM HAYES CENTER, NEBRASKA, TO PREPARE THE CITY ORDINANCE

She brought the idea to the board of trustees. In harmonious rapport and unwavering faith, they worked to pass an ordinance making Hayes Center a sanctuary city for protection of the unborn.

PRIMAVERA SIGNS PAPERWORK TO MAKE HAYES CENTER A SANCTUARY CITY FOR PROTECTION OF THE UNBORN

"There are people who complain and ridicule, but there is more good fruit," said Primavera. "Even those who have moved away from Hayes Center are telling us how blessed and proud they are that the ordinance was passed. They have pride in the city, which is important. Also, a town two hours east of us, called Blue Hill, heard about the ordinance being passed and passed their own ordinance a week after ours. That's fruit that we know of; we may never know the full impact this has made. This is setting an example for young people. The next generation is learning when life begins, what abortion is and does. They are not turning a blind eye to reality and humanity."

Prayer paved the way for this sanctuary city ordinance in Hayes Center. "There is power in prayer and unity," Primavera said. "I believe the ordinance passed so easily because of our prayer meetings. Once a month, we committed to pray for an hour. All denominations joined together. We were united; we had a focus. I believe God honored the prayers and unity," Primavera said. In Lubbock, Texas, similar unified prayer efforts preceded their vote to become a sanctuary city for the unborn.

ENGAGE:

Agree with two or three others to set up a meeting once a month to pray specifically for sanctuary cities, and in particular for the Lord to make your own municipality one such refuge for preborn human life.

AN AERIAL VIEW OF LANDS IRRIGATED FROM THE OGALLALA AQUIFER, IN KANSAS

19

REPENTANCE HEALS THE LAND

By Aaron Mercer

In our churches, we often hear cries for healing. Our hearts yearn for restoration of peace and health in our homes, our neighborhoods, and our nation. But are we willing to do the work God wants in preparation for that healing?

Ambassador Sam Brownback was willing. And he saw God heal the actual land of his state. Growing up on a family farm in Kansas, Brownback has always understood the land. One matter particularly important to him is the preservation of the Ogallala Aquifer. This massive underground source of water extends for more than 175,000 square miles across eight states. It is a key reason why western Kansas, which receives relatively little precipitation, can nevertheless be a breadbasket for the rest of the country.

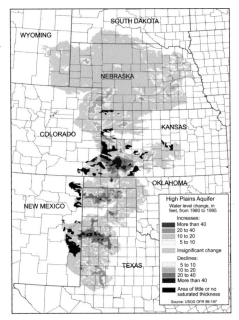

A MAP OF THE HIGH PLAINS/OGALLALA AQUIFER REVEALS THE STARK DECLINE IN WATER LEVELS FOR KANSAS FROM 1980 TO 1995. THOSE LEVELS BEGAN RECOVERING ABOUT THE TIME BROWNBACK BECAME GOVERNOR IN 2011

For years as a state and federal official, Brownback was confronted with alarming statistics about how overuse was depleting the Ogallala. Then, after he became governor of Kansas, something remarkable happened. "The head of the Kansas Geological Survey comes into my office," Brownback told IFA. "He said, 'This is really odd, but that aquifer is recharging faster than we thought.'"

This was supposed to be impossible, but suddenly there was a real chance for farmers to use the aquifer sustainably. Brownback attributed this blessed opportunity to a deeper healing.

GOV. BROWNBACK SPEAKING AT THE GROUNDBREAKING CEREMONY FOR MCCONNELL AIR FORCE BASE IN WICHITA, KANSAS, IN 2014

"The greed was lifted off of the land," he said. Brownback came to this conclusion after confronting an unseen but very real — and very deep — stain on our nation. Native American intercessors Jay Swallow and Negiel Bigpond, along with Christian leaders like author Cindy Jacobs, had helped him explore the depths of our nation's wrongs against American Indians, and Brownback had acted. Greed, he realized, had motivated settlers to take land that wasn't theirs to take.

BEFORE BEING ELECTED THE 46TH GOVERNOR OF KANSAS, BROWNBACK SERVED AS A REPRESENTATIVE IN CONGRESS AND THEN AS A SENATOR. HERE IS SEN. BROWNBACK IN 2005

While serving in the U.S. Senate, Brownback authored an official apology to Native Americans in 2004 (Senate Joint Resolution 37). That resolution acknowledged the U.S. government's breaking of treaties, the theft of tribal resources, and the resultant ongoing social and economic troubles of American Indians. After five years in which Brownback fought to build support, the resolution was attached as an amendment to a broader package and signed into law by President Obama.

THE POTAWATOMI TRAIL OF DEATH WAS THE FORCED REMOVAL BY MILITIA OF NEARLY 900 MEMBERS OF THE POTAWATOMI NATION. DURING THE 61-DAY, 660-MILE TREK FROM TWIN LAKES, INDIANA; TO OSAWATOMIE, KANSAS; OVER 40 DIED, MOSTLY CHILDREN

That was a landmark moment, but Brownback sought more. When he became governor, he publicly took the spirit of this apology to key communities that had experienced hurt. In 2013, this included the end point of the Potawatomi tribe's Trail of Death, in Kansas. Swallow participated in many of these ceremonies, and Brownback remembers him saying: "OK, it's finished. It's done." Swallow's prophetic word meant that these penitence efforts had led to a healing in the land.

VIEW OF A SUNSET OVER A WHEAT FIELD IN KANSAS

Brownback, known more recently for his leadership in advancing international religious freedom, is keeping up reconciliation efforts with Native Americans nationwide. IFA President and CEO Dave Kubal and other IFA staff members joined him at one such ceremony on the National Day of Prayer. During a sidebar conversation, Brownback told IFA that the wrongs committed against Native Americans, African Americans, and prenatal victims of abortion "are three strands of poison" defiling our land. Truly, we do need healing.

(TOP LEFT) BROWNBACK SERVED AS U.S. AMBASSADOR-AT-LARGE FOR INTERNATIONAL RELIGIOUS FREEDOM UNDER PRESIDENT TRUMP FROM 2018 TO 2021. (RIGHT) IFA'S DAVE KUBAL HONORS BROWNBACK AT AN IFA PRAYER EVENT IN 2021

In Scripture, God tells King Solomon: *"... if my people who are called by my name humble themselves, and pray and seek my face and turn from their wicked ways, then I will hear from heaven and will forgive their sin and heal their land"* (2 Chronicles 7:14). As governor of

Kansas, U.S. senator, and government ambassador, Brownback has strived to fulfill God's conditions. And God is sure to keep His promise.

IN 2021, DOZENS OF CHRISTIAN LEADERS GATHERED AT THE CONGRESSIONAL CEMETERY, IN WASHINGTON, D.C., ON THE MORNING OF THE NATIONAL DAY OF PRAYER TO OFFER AND RECEIVE FORGIVENESS FOR THE ATROCITIES COMMITTED AGAINST NATIVE AMERICANS. FORMER AMBASSADOR, GOVERNOR, AND SENATOR SAM BROWNBACK READ THE PROCLAMATION THAT PRESIDENT OBAMA SIGNED INTO LAW IN 2009. ON HAND TO RECEIVE THE APOLOGY WERE DR. NEGIEL BIGPOND, A FULL-BLOOD MEMBER OF THE EUCHEE (YUCHI) INDIAN TRIBE, AND MARY FAUS, REPRESENTING THE OJIBWAY AND CREE TRIBES. IN THE PHOTO, FROM LEFT: NATIONAL DAY OF PRAYER PRESIDENT KATHY BRANZELL; DR. BIGPOND; BROWNBACK; AND FAUS

ENGAGE:

Ask the Lord to raise up many more officials and statesmen like Sam Brownback — men and women with a heart after God's own — and pray for a deep healing of this land.

FIRST CENTURY CHRISTIAN MARKINGS ETCHED OVER EGYPTIAN TEMPLE CARVINGS

20

SHERRIE MOORE:
FOLLOWING THE LAMB

By Wanda Alger and Judy McDonough

Truly, only the Lord God can make "a highway of worship and reconciliation" into Egypt through Virginia — by moving upon ordinary believers to begin praying for people they barely know even exist.

Matthew and Sherrie Moore had been called to Richmond, Virginia, in 1992 from the Northern Virginia area. The couple had no idea then what was to unfold, or anything about the story they were to become part of while serving a local Messianic Jewish congregation. But that story began when they got connected to other local ministries that desired to see a spirit of oneness among the churches. Through those ministries, the Moores began hearing stories about decades of prayer and of advances toward church unity in Richmond.

In the 1970s, there was a movement among pastors and leaders who gathered to worship across racial lines. One elderly pastor with whom Sherrie spoke recalled how beautiful that worship was as people of different races and backgrounds grasped hands under the banner of the one true King. Pastors began exchanging Sunday morning pulpit times with each other.

The next move of God the Moores became aware of was a prayer mobilization in the 1980s. Richmond had the No. 1 murder rate per capita in the nation at that time (see chapter 11 of this book for a powerful testimony about that). The prayer mobilization eventually waned, but the hearts of those in the city continued to desire a unified expression, and pastoral and ministry leaders kept gathering in small numbers, maintaining a vision for "the Church of Richmond."

SHERRIE AND MATTHEW MOORE: 'REGULAR PEOPLE... NOBODY FANTASTIC OTHER THAN WE SAID YES TO JESUS'

A Search for Willing Followers of the Lamb

In 1996, the Lord awakened Sherrie one morning and told her it was time to gather the intercessors of the city. She and Matthew had a list of 30 people who liked to pray. So, they made a flyer and mailed it out. The night before the gathering, Sherrie received a vision in which she saw a lamb wearing a dog collar and leash; she was walking with the lamb in tow, and saying: "Everywhere my foot treads, you have given me." Then she saw a new scene: a lamb unfettered, and she and others were voluntarily walking behind the lamb. The Lord then said: "I am looking for those that will follow the Lamb, not lead the Lamb. Joshua went where I led him to go." This was an invitation to listen carefully to the Lord's strategies in intercession. He knows how to lock and unlock, thought Sherrie, and this was the message she was to share at the gathering.

The night of that first gathering, in January 1997, those 30 flyers had assembled some 220 people from all over the city. This was God's time to get the city's attention again, and so another prayer mobilization began. But the participants would need to "follow the Lamb."

EARLY CITYWIDE GATHERINGS DREW CHRISTIANS FROM EVERY DENOMINATION, LANGUAGE, AND CULTURE FOR UNITED PRAYER

These citywide gatherings grew and continued for several years, helping to build relationships and testimonies among the Body of Christ. Wherever there was denominational unity, the higher calling was to focus on tribes, tongues, and nations (ethnicities) — not on the denominations. Many of these gatherings began looking like the United

Nations, with Christians from multiple cultures and languages joining together in unified prayer. In December 1998, the Lord gave Matthew a vision for day-and-night worship — for the city, and by the city.

After a few months, city leaders asked for a confirmation of this vision. And that day they received a brochure announcing the launch of a 24/7 worship and prayer room in Kansas City, called International House of Prayer (IHOP). Matthew and two others went on a "fact-finding" mission, because none of them had ever heard of this group before. They returned knowing that God indeed wanted to establish a day-and-night worship and prayer center in the heart of their city. Thus was born the Richmond International House of Prayer (RIHOP).

For the next seven years, RIHOP was hosted by local churches, but in 2006 the ministry moved into its own facility. The teams represented were multi-congregational and multi-ethnic, and together they prayed for Richmond and for the nation. By 2011 there was an increasing

IN 2006, THE RICHMOND INTERNATIONAL HOUSE OF PRAYER (RIHOP) WAS STARTED, IN A FACILITY LOCATED IN SHOCKOE BOTTOM, ONE OF THE OLDEST NEIGHBORHOODS IN RICHMOND, WHERE THIS DIVERSE PRAYER GATHERING WOULD OPERATE FOR THE NEXT TEN YEARS

prayer burden to reach the regional Muslim community, as interfaith prayer rooms on local college campuses were becoming almost entirely. Islamic, and this population was growing exponentially.

In 2015 Sherrie was in the prayer room reading Genesis 50, the account of Jacob dying in Egypt. As she read, she sensed the Lord stopping her to have her begin praying for Egypt. The time of the Isaiah 19:23 highway had already begun, she perceived He was saying, and then He told her that there would be "a bridge" between Richmond and this highway, and that people would be traveling back and forth on it. Sherrie sensed the Lord saying also that the voice of the Egyptian people was very important. At that time, however, though she knew there were Egyptian people living in her city, she did not personally know any of them.

God's Heart for Egypt

The team at RIHOP began to pray. Two weeks later, during a 24-hour time of multi-congregational worship, Sherrie received a message on the RIHOP Facebook page: *"My name is Wael, from Egypt, we have prayer in our church ... how can we communicate and partner together to help build an Arabic-speaking house of prayer?"* Sherrie promptly responded to the message and then met with the pastor and the leadership a few days later. There,

IN 2015, AFTER SHERRIE HAD PRAYED FOR EGYPT, GOD DIVINELY CONNECTED HER AND PASTOR AGAYBY, IN RICHMOND

she learned that the Egyptian community in the Richmond area was approximately 3,000 strong. Sherrie and Pastor Agayby, of the Egyptian church, exchanged stories of their personal journeys to Richmond. Pastor Agayby had a huge ministry in Egypt, with many of his spiritual sons there starting up churches of their own. As it happened, he'd received a word from the Lord in 2006 (the year RIHOP moved to its own facility) that he was to relocate to Richmond. After four years of prayer, he finally arrived in the U.S. Things were very difficult for him here — so much so that by 2011, he'd begun packing to

ON SHERRIE'S FIRST TRIP TO EGYPT, IN 2018, A SIGN IN A CHURCH DISPLAYED ISAIAH 19:25, THE SAME SCRIPTURE GOD USED TO SPEAK TO HER ABOUT RICHMOND'S 'BRIDGE TO THE ISAIAH 19 HIGHWAY'

return to Egypt. But meanwhile, the Lord had reached out to a local Baptist pastor in a dream, telling him to make a way for Pastor Agayby to stay in Richmond. This was the exact time that RIHOP had received an increased burden to begin praying for the Islamic community — and specifically for Egyptians and for Egypt.

In 2017, the Lord reminded Sherrie of the bridge He'd mentioned, from Richmond to the Isaiah 19:23–25 highway: *In that day there will be a highway from Egypt to Assyria, and Assyria will come into Egypt, and Egypt into Assyria, and the Egyptians will worship with the Assyrians. In that day Israel will be the third with Egypt and Assyria, a blessing in the midst of the earth, whom the LORD of hosts has blessed, saying, "Blessed be Egypt my people, and Assyria the work of my hands, and Israel my inheritance."*

Sherrie and her team had to learn to pray without envisioning what it would look like when God answered. Sometimes, we can miss how God is answering our prayers by envisioning in our minds what His answer will look like. This lesson was further imprinted on her when the Lord opened a door for her to travel to Israel and then to Egypt.

God gave Sherrie great favor in Egypt. She spoke at churches there, sharing about God's heart for the Egyptians and how God was raising them up to go to the nations and preach the gospel to the unreached, with many Muslims coming to the Lord through their obedience. Sherrie also saw that there was great revival coming to Egypt. From 2017 to 2019 she and Pastor Agayby and Wael traveled to Egypt several times, reaching out to other pastors and also to widows, prisoners'

HELPING HOUSEHOLDS RAISE GOATS TO SELL FOR MEAT, AND BAKING BREAD FOR SALE AT MARKET (RIGHT), ARE EXAMPLES OF THE MANY MICRO-BUSINESSES CREATED BY JEWELS OF THE NILE

wives and children, and at-risk girls. During this time, Sherrie started up Jewels of the Nile and has overseen creation of 170 micro-businesses among the poorest in Egypt, impacting communities from Cairo to Asyut. Sherrie had the privilege of addressing houses of prayer throughout Egypt. Indeed, she was even asked to dedicate one such house of prayer, newly birthed in a city outside of Al Minya.

Little did Sherrie know that while she was traveling from Richmond to Egypt, God was at work expanding the story. He instructed her to go to a gathering in Cyprus called Isaiah 19. She did not know anyone at this conference, so she recruited a friend, and in November 2018 went to Cyprus.

'Hurled Into the Nations'

At that conference, she had a vision in which she saw people being hurled from the nations into the land surrounding the Fertile Crescent. In essence, she saw "the Isaiah 19 highway," and she asked the Lord to explain what she was seeing. He said He was sending witnesses from the nations. "Witnesses to what?" Sherrie asked. *"Witnesses of the rapid advancement of My kingdom and the return of My Son,"* she heard Him respond. Then, she audibly heard: *"And R.A. Martinez will be used mightily to fill these houses of prayer."* Sherrie had known Martinez casually over the years; he lived in another city in Virginia. She found it a bit awkward to reach out to him with this word, but she did it anyway. His response was gracious, but Sherrie had no way of knowing that God had already given him a burden to "fill houses of prayer" in those same geographic locations.

In February 2019, Sherrie received a call from Martinez: The Lord had spoken to his team about moving the ministry to another city. They had a list of five cities under consideration, including Atlanta, New York, and Kansas City; Richmond was No. 5 on the list. The ministry members wanted to move to where there was an existing house of prayer, and they had been in contact with leaders from those cities. Sherrie did not know much about what they were doing, but she agreed to be open.

ONERS' WIVES AND THEIR CHILDREN IN EL MINYA, EGYPT

lay fast that Martinez and his small team were engaged ıders had a dream. In the dream, the Lord showed that ımond, and He said: *"You will be all right if you park parking space."* When the dreamer awoke, she heard *Moore."* At the time, the dreamer thought this may be one she knew in college, as she otherwise had no idea ʼe was. She recounted the dream and what she'd heard ıe team, and Martinez then knew exactly where they were to move.

In mid-2019, MAPS (originally, Missions and Prayer School) moved to Richmond and "adopted" RIHOP, and Sherrie became one of the leaders of MAPS. The work exploded in a few years, increasing in ministry scope and expanding to almost 100 staff members and three overseas bases in Eurasia, the Middle East, and the Levant. These bases are houses of prayer, and teams go back and forth from Richmond to "the Isaiah 19 highway" and beyond.

God has enabled MAPS Global, as it is called today, to move onto a 60,000-square-foot campus facility across 6 acres. Through the prayers of the intercessors at both RIHOP and MAPS, God has prepared a people for a city, and a city for a people. Prospects from all over the country are brought in for training in Richmond and then "hurled into" the nations — and especially into the nations of the Muslim world.

INSIDE THE PRAYER ROOM ON THE CAMPUS OF MAPS GLOBAL, IN RICHMOND, VIRGINIA

In this expanding work, the MAPS Global and RIHOP Global Prayer Room is moving toward establishing seven bases in the 10/40 Window: the rectangular region of North Africa, the Middle East, and Asia located between 10 and 40 degrees north latitude. The area has been called The Resistant Belt, where the majority of the world's Muslims, Hindus, and Buddhists live. This ground is being prepared through the prayers of intercessors who are "following the Lamb" in Richmond and two other cities.

We all move forward in the glorious things of our God, but this is never without challenge. In 2006, just when RIHOP received the key to its building, Matthew was diagnosed with inoperable cancer. For ten years the Moores prayed fervently about this, in fellowship with multiple congregations in Richmond and around the world. In 2016, Matthew went home to Christ. Sherrie has learned not to be shaken by the things of this world. She told the Lord she would bow to His sovereignty "and live in the mystery of not knowing why." Sherrie said, "God is Who He says He is, no matter what," said

SHERRIE AND MATTHEW IN 2009

Sherrie. "Circumstances do not change the nature of God."

It's apparent that through Sherrie's and Matthew's obedience and the faithful prayers of united believers, God has brought about an amazing kingdom partnership. And this divine appointment resulted in the merging of two spiritual families from two very different countries and cultures, by which He opened wide a door for the gospel and for the expansion of His kingdom.

That's what God can do with even a single intercessor who responds to the promptings of His Spirit to pray for people the intercessor may not even know.

ENGAGE:

Might there be something about which the Lord has been speaking to you, something new and untried, but about which you sense a prompting to seek His direction? Listen closely, and be willing to step out — even if slowly at first and with small steps.

21

BIBLES IN SCHOOLS

By Gloria Robles

Hannah Sailsbury, a public school teacher, began walking the school hallways and praying silently for the other teachers and the students. "I prayed for their salvation and that those who knew Jesus would be bold in their faith," Sailsbury said. "One day I prayed that Jesus' name would be spoken in the hallways and classrooms of my school. Jesus soon answered that prayer in bigger ways than I could have imagined."

Sailsbury noticed that a second-grade boy in her reading group was reading an old Bible from the school library. After the 8-year-old had read something to her from out of that Bible, he said something powerfully moving: "I want to learn more about God, heaven, and hell."

Stunned, Sailsbury perceived in her heart at that very moment this Holy Spirit–inspired thought: *What if Bibles at the children's reading level were available in public school libraries?*

And so, Sailsbury was divinely led to found Bibles in Schools, of which she is executive director.

HANNAH SAILSBURY WITH STUDENTS HOLDING COPIES OF *THE ACTION BIBLE* AND *THE ACTION BIBLE: HEROES AND VILLAINS,* WHICH ARE DONATED TO SCHOOL LIBRARIES ACROSS THE NATION THROUGH THE BIBLES IN SCHOOLS PROGRAM

Bibles in Schools exists primarily to place children's Bibles in public school libraries, so that they're available for checkout by the children. What has come as something of a surprise is that through this ministry, the word of God is touching not just those young students, but also some of their teachers — and even some of the administrators and educators responsible for reviewing donated books for approval.

To be sure, this is a ministry whose time has come. And though we've seen distressing levels of acceptance among school officials and even parents (!) for distribution of LGBTQ-centric and even pornographic materials in public schools, the mere mention of Bibles for school kids is frequently met with stunning hostility. One school superintendent in Alabama — a state in which the acceptance rate for this Bible-distribution ministry is only about 9% — actually forbade his staff, in no uncertain terms, to accept any Bibles.

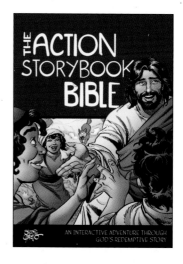

Even so, there has also been much to celebrate, and the Lord is powerfully using the Bible in Schools ministry. After Sailsbury appeared on an IFA webcast, intercessors responded with astonishing eagerness. An 87-year-old woman in South Carolina bought 60 copies of *The Action Bible* — and then reached out to Bibles in Schools for help with the process of getting those Bibles into her local schools. She set up meetings with school librarians, one of whom was very excited for the opportunity, because it happened that her library had just thrown away some very old, moldy Bibles. Now, this librarian was happily requesting multiple copies of *The Action Bible*.

In further good news, an IFA intercessor in South Dakota went directly to her school superintendent, who approved Bibles for the schools there. One library in Illinois actually had a waiting list for Bibles! IFA intercessor Lori read about Bibles in Schools at IFApray.org and got busy calling up schools in her home state of California. One of her friends is a school librarian who was more than happy to help out.

In fact, just before Lori contacted this friend, the local school had received some books promoting LGBTQ ideas, which were to be placed in the library. The librarian was thrilled that she could put Bibles on the shelves as well. This school and four others received Bibles as a result.

A librarian in Massachusetts said Bibles haven't been checked out in his high school library for the past five years. When he put copies of *The Action Bible* on the shelf, however, they were checked out immediately!

Bibles in Schools reached out to all the librarians in one Virginia county by email but received no response. The town sheriff, however, acted quickly by phoning up a school board member. Within hours, the school board had decided to accept Bibles for all 19 schools in its districts.

And this need is great even beyond the schools: A juvenile detention center in Texas reached out to Bibles in Schools. A representative said that in the 11 years she has worked there, no one had ever donated

Bibles to the center, which can house up to 126 kids.

Our God is powerfully at work even in and through the very youngest among us. A student from Florida recently wrote the ministry: *"Hi, my name is Matthew. I am in 7th grade. I am working on a writing assignment about one of my core beliefs. My core belief is that Bibles should be read and available to all children in schools. In my research, I found your website. How can I get this started in Tampa?"*

In just a few years, Bibles in Schools donated more than 10,000 Bibles to upwards of 2,250 schools. And it all started with Sailsbury's silent and solitary prayer walks through public school hallways. Again and again, God shows us that He is able to take a single seed and bring forth an astonishing and abundant harvest for His glory and the saving of many souls.

ENGAGE:

Wherever you are and whatever the Lord has you doing, ask Him to give you eyes to see beyond the surface, to discern the "hidden" things — the needs both practical and spiritual of those among whom you live, work, and pray.

I will take my stand at my watchpost and station myself on the tower, and look out to see what he will say to me ... (Habakkuk 2:1).

Blessed is the one who listens to me, watching daily at my gates, waiting beside my doors (Proverbs 8:34).

Restore to me the joy of your salvation and grant me a willing spirit, to sustain me (Psalm 51:12 NIV).

PART 4: POWERFUL PRAYER WARRIORS

What makes a "powerful prayer warrior"? Is it an intrinsic quality of a particular person? Is it a personality type or the result of education? Is it only for a special class of Christian? No. The power comes from God, as does the warrior spirit, grown in a willing servant of the Lord Jesus Christ.

KING'S COLLEGE, CAMBRIDGE UNIVERSITY, WHERE DEREK PRINCE STUDIED ANCIENT AND MODERN PHILOSOPHY

22

DEREK PRINCE: 'TEACHER OF THE SCRIPTURES'

By IFA Staff

Derek Prince was a scholar of Greek and Latin at Eton College and Cambridge University, and he held degrees in ancient and modern philosophy. He also studied Aramaic at Cambridge, as well as Hebrew at both Cambridge and The Hebrew University of Jerusalem. A self-described atheist with a colorful personal history, Derek took up the Bible as a mere "study" (he considered the Bible a "philosophical work"), but he ended up experiencing a supernatural encounter with Jesus Christ.

Derek went on to become one of the world's most influential Bible teachers. A defining moment in his life came when he received a word from the Lord in 1941 regarding the coming move of God: "It shall be like a little stream. The little stream shall become a river. The river shall become a great river. The great river shall become a sea. The sea shall become a mighty ocean, and it shall be through thee: But how, thou must not know, thou canst not know, thou shall not know."

DEREK PRINCE PREACHING AT TRINITY CHURCH (NOW KNOWN AS CORNERSTONE CHURCH) IN SAN ANTONIO, TEXAS, IN 1974

Then, in 1944, while stationed in Israel, he heard: "You are called to be a teacher of the Scriptures, in truth and faith and love, which are in Christ Jesus — for many." These words of the Lord came to define Derek's ministry, which continues to reach people in nearly every nation even today, all these decades after his death.

In 1973, three years after speaking at the 350th anniversary of the landing of the Mayflower, in Plymouth, Massachusetts, Derek published *Shaping History Through Prayer & Fasting*. Given his recently gained insights on the spiritual focus of the Pilgrims, Derek was keen to bring that emphasis to attendees at the Florida

THE *MAYFLOWER II*, A REPLICA OF THE 17TH-CENTURY SHIP THE PILGRIMS SAILED TO AMERICA

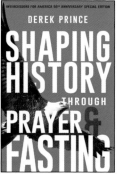

conference that led to the formation of IFA. In addition, the Supreme Court's Roe v. Wade decision, handed down in January of that year, was heavy upon the hearts of the conference speakers and participants. Toward the close of the conference, attendees were given an opportunity to express interest in following up. Many did, and from among these, a small number were selected by the conference organizers to take the next steps. The members of this group, which included Derek, became the founders of IFA.

Derek taught that good government is God's will, because it provides a climate for the gospel to be preached. Once Derek obtained American citizenship, he studied the U.S. Constitution and became convinced that its

THE ORIGINAL 1973 EDITION OF *SHAPING HISTORY THROUGH PRAYER & FASTING* (TOP), BY DEREK PRINCE, WHICH WAS REPUBLISHED IN 2023 (MIDDLE) FOR IFA'S 50TH ANNIVERSARY. ABOVE, IFA CO-FOUNDER JOHN BECKETT HOLDS HIS ORIGINAL COPY OF *SHAPING HISTORY THROUGH PRAYER & FASTING*, SIGNED BY EACH OF IFA'S FOUNDING MEMBERS IN 1973

THE GRAVE OF DEREK PRINCE, IN JERUSALEM

drafters' objectives fulfill Paul's admonition to Timothy: *that we may lead a quiet and peaceable life in all godliness and honesty* (KJ21). He came to see that their desire was that we as Americans should be thankful and vigilant in praying over a founding charter that aligns so well with the purposes and principles of human government as ordained in Scripture. This teaching is fundamental to the mission of IFA.

Indeed, all who are linked to IFA owe a debt of gratitude to Derek Prince, for without his vision and encouragement, it is unlikely that we would even exist today. Certainly, the prayer movement worldwide would be much the poorer.

Derek summed up his life's teaching in three words: *"God is faithful."*

IFA INTERCESSORS AT A PRAYER EVENT IN WASHINGTON, D.C.

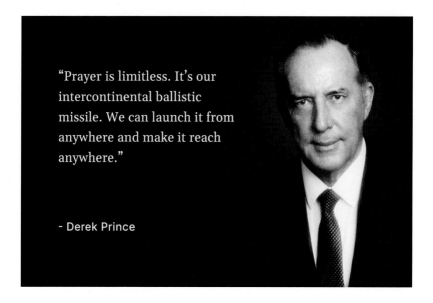

"Prayer is limitless. It's our intercontinental ballistic missile. We can launch it from anywhere and make it reach anywhere."

- Derek Prince

ENGAGE:

What words might you use to sum up your own life in Christ? Consider the ways Jesus has already changed your life and guided your prayers, and reflect on what He might be leading you to do from this point.

RIVERS AND MOUNTAINS FORM THE BEAUTIFUL LANDSCAPE OF WESTERN PENNSYLVANIA

23

BETSY WEST: DISCOVERING BURIED TREASURE

By Betsy West

I have lived in Washington, Pennsylvania, all my life. My ancestors fought in the American Revolutionary War and were among the early settlers of our area. Still, I could never identify any significant achievement or historical mark within my community. By the time I was an adult, the city was in decline, and there seemed to be no likelihood of any improvement.

When my husband, Bill, and I became believers in Christ, God supernaturally pulled us from the brink of divorce and marked us for eternity. Now that we were saved and Spirit-filled, it was as if God had put us in hyperdrive, we were so hungry for the Lord. That was when we started going to a prayer meeting at our local church.

In 1998, we discovered "city reaching" and the Lighthouse of Prayer movement. We began prayer-walking through our city. As we walked and prayed, joined by others in our multi-denominational fellowship, we noticed for the first time in our lives that there was a church building on nearly every street corner in our city. Most of these churches could in our city. Most of these churches could easily seat 400 people or more, and yet the congregations at that time typically numbered about 50 each, or fewer. Even in the rural areas of our county, numerous churches, just as large as those in the city, stood

BETSY AND BILL WEST

within sight of one another upon the hilltops. What had happened in this place?

Answers to our questions and prayers began emerging in 2001, when our local Historical Society found a box filled with written historical

accounts of the first 100 years of our county, including copies of speeches given on the day of the centennial celebration, in 1881. One of those accounts changed our perspective on the community forever. The Rev. I.N. Hays offered the religious history of Washington

County, an account that caused our hearts to overflow as we began seeing our county through the eyes of the heavenly Father — our true heritage, hidden for a century but now revealed by the grace of God through this resurrected history.

That was only the tip of the iceberg, however: Within the account's 19 pages, we discovered that this county had been born amid a great outpouring of the Holy Spirit, preceded by intense intercessory prayer.

As Rev. Hays explained: *"This county was brought into existence in the midst of revivals. It is just one hundred years since God first poured out his spirit upon this western county and made sacred the spot where we stand. In the fall of 1781, the churches of Chartiers and Pigeon Creek, under the care of Dr. John McMillan, and Upper Buffalo and Cross Creek, under the care of Rev. Joseph Smith, were simultaneously made glad with the divine presence, and from that day to this the cloud of heavenly benediction has never been lifted from this garden spot of earth.*

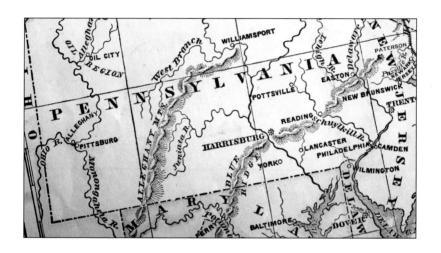

"[T]he first revival of religion ever witnessed west of the Allegheny mountains took place in the fall of the year 1781, simultaneous with the organization of this county. ... This work seems to have been preceded and ushered in, on the one hand, by deep groanings on the part of God's people over the very low state of religious feeling among themselves ... and on the other by the frequent Sabbath and week-night meetings held for preaching, prayer and exhortation. Not unfrequently these services were continued throughout the entire night, even before there were any wide-spread demonstrations of the Spirit's presence. ...

"The season of awakening continued for some five or six years. ... During the latter part of 1801 there was a wide-spread feeling of distress at the 'low state of religion' amongst God's people and the alarming increase in the boldness and out-spoken opposition of the enemies of Christ. Intense, secret prayer of the people of Three Springs,

a part of Rev. Elisha McCurdy's charge, spent from sun-setting on Thursday for an outpouring of the Spirit at their approaching communion season, to take place on the 4th Sabbath of September, 1802.

"The time came. The windows of heaven were opened. ... Thursday being observed as a day of fasting and prayer, gave increased evidence of the Spirit's presence. Before the sermon had commenced, two young persons, who had retired to the woods to pray, fell prostrate on the ground, completely overcome. It was the commencement of the falling exercise. 'We were exposed to the wrath of God.' When urged to look to Christ they said: 'We have so long rejected the offer of mercy and our hearts have become so hard, that we fear God will not have mercy upon us.' ... Great numbers were prostrate on the ground utterly helpless, and as the next day began to dawn, light began to break into many souls which up to this time had been left in total darkness."

There is so much more detail to this account to share. On one occasion during that great outpouring, more than 10,000 people from the sparsely settled country areas assembled together for weeks. Imagine this: no roads or public conveyances of any kind, without shelter or any accommodation except whatever they had happened to bring with them.

Dr. John McMillan, educated at Princeton Theological Seminary, recorded that one evening, instead of going to the dining hall, he retired to his room. A bright light invaded the room, and he knew that he must go to the "Western frontier" to preach the gospel. Washington County was "the frontier" at that time, with the Ohio River being its western boundary. McMillan then recruited Joseph Smith and a few others to join him in this endeavor. He knew he could have taken a very profitable position at any of the established churches within the Colonies, but that he had instead the express call to serve on this rugged frontier.

This was not only a revival — it was a documented move of God that influenced the culture with reformation and impacted our government, our churches, and our families. This small book of his recorded the elements of true and accurate intercession: individual intercession; corporate prayer and fasting; and persistent, passionate crying out to God to revisit our land. The focused prayer resulted in an outpouring that was *"nothing short of Pentecost."*

Verifiable, measurable evidence that God had tabernacled with Washington County for many years lay hidden until 2001. After multiple congregations interceded together for our desolate community, God answered our prayers by stirring up faith and hope through the testimony of those who had gone before us.

STEEPLES DOT THE HORIZON IN A PANORAMIC VIEW OF WASHINGTON, PENNSYLVANIA

PASTOR JOE JEFFERYS STANDS AT THE SITE WHERE OVER 10,000 PEOPLE GATHERED DURING THE GREAT REVIVAL OF 1782 ON PENNSYLVANIA'S WESTERN FRONTIER

This revelation inspired us to pray in bold new ways for breakthroughs in our community. One of the leaders of our efforts was Pastor Joe Jefferys of the Upper Buffalo Presbyterian Church, where the revival history was discovered. We worked with him on several communitywide events to bring intercessors to this special place. A rainbow appeared during a time of prayer walking — but there had been no rain at all! We were also there one evening when the northern lights appeared, again, with no warning and no media announcement ahead of time that such a phenomenon was to occur. We knew we had once again been "kissed by the Son."

Every IFA intercessor is part of something eternal. In the words of Rev. Hays:

"Just as a little child may strike the flint which may kindle a fire on yonder mountain top, from which shall go forth rays of light piercing the utmost ether; so there are lines of influence which shall go on widening and extending, until, touching the shores of time, the receding wave shall give to the recording angel, what only in eternity we will be able fully to know or comprehend."

ENGAGE:

Perhaps through research you can discover something in the history of your county, town, or city that you can begin using to drive your intercessions with greater urgency and power.

24

JOHN TALCOTT JR.:
PRAYER AND FASTING PIONEER

By IFA Staff

"Let us remember that by praying and fasting with God's people for our nation, we present a channel through which God can work." — John Talcott Jr.

John G. Talcott Jr., IFA's first president, was a "road builder" who lived to be 105 (Feb. 26, 1908–May 27, 2013). We who follow upon the foundations he laid are empowered by the legacy he leaves. Road builders are the "blood, sweat, and tears" people who forge the pathway, clear the debris, level the surface, and bear the heat of the day. When the road builders are finished, the travelers can move along swiftly, enjoying a smooth surface, though rarely thinking of the debt they owe the builders. This very building and pioneering heritage was John's throughout his active life.

John was, by vocation, a prosperous cranberry producer in Plymouth, Massachusetts. He served as a board member of Ocean Spray Cranberries, Inc., and of Gordon-Conwell Theological Seminary (along with Dr. Billy Graham). He was not only a successful businessman, but also a fervent Christian and an intense patriot, one who was very knowledgeable about our nation's founding.

TALCOTT'S LOVE FOR THE HISTORY OF BIBLICAL FAITH IN AMERICA LED HIM TO BE VERY ACTIVE IN HIS HOMETOWN. HE SERVED AS CHAIRMAN FOR THE 350TH COMMITTEE TO HONOR THE PILGRIMS LANDING, FOUNDED THE PLYMOUTH ROCK FOUNDATION, AND WAS AN ACTIVE MEMBER OF THE PILGRIM SOCIETY - ALL BEFORE HE WAS 62-YEARS OLD, AS PICTURED HERE DURING PLYMOUTH'S 350TH CELEBRATION

Starting in 1975, he was instrumental in calling the nation to fast on the first Friday of every month, a ministry that continues at IFA to this day. John once wrote: "When our hearts are contrite before the Lord, our prayer life becomes more effective. Isaiah 58:4 tells us a fast is 'to make your voice heard on high.' With increased sensitivity in prayer, a time of fasting should be an opportunity to pray for mercy in a time of impending divine judgment (see Jonah 3:5–10). For our nation, at this time, this aspect of fasting is especially important."

Asked why such pursuits are so important, John replied in an interview: "It seems as though one thing we don't really recognize any longer is that our Founders had a vision of building the nation for God's purposes. Many had a strong faith and a determination to live for Him. That's possibly the answer.

FOR YEARS, TALCOTT SERVED AS PARADE MARSHALL FOR PLYMOUTH'S ANNUAL FOURTH OF JULY PARADE. IN 2008, HE MARCHED IN FULL MILITARY UNIFORM AT THE AGE OF 100

People today go along seeking the comfortable things in life rather than the purposes of God. Many people do not seem to have real faith awakened. We must take care to see that we don't become preoccupied with the niceties of this world and lose sight of the fact that this world is not our permanent home. If we are not living for the purposes of God, we're just wasting away a lifetime."

IN 2004, A 96-YEAR-OLD TALCOTT (LEFT) LED THE OLD COLONY CLUB'S ANNUAL FOREFATHERS DAY PROCESSIONAL BEFORE DAWN IN PLYMOUTH, MASSACHUSETTS. DR. PAUL JEHLE (RIGHT), EXECUTIVE DIRECTOR OF THE PLYMOUTH ROCK FOUNDATION, SAID OF HIS FRIEND AND MENTOR: "JOHN DID MORE AFTER THE AGE OF 75 THAN MOST PEOPLE DO IN A LIFETIME"

John well understood our nation's Pilgrim and Puritan foundations, and with good reason: He was of Puritan and *Mayflower* Pilgrim ancestry himself. He could trace his descent from Pilgrim John Chilton, of the *Mayflower*, and his ancestors were also a part of the migration that established the Connecticut Colony under the leadership of Thomas Hooker. And John knew that if Americans would cling to the righteousness these foundations represent, it would bring national blessing. "If we forget how we got here," he said, "if that is forsaken — then all is lost."

100-YEAR-OLD TALCOTT HONORS AMERICA'S PILGRIM FOREFATHERS WITH A SALUTE IN FRONT OF PLYMOUTH'S PILGRIM HALL DURING THE PARADE

Sally Fesperman, a long-time IFA board member and close friend of the Talcotts, recalls that John wanted us to ask the important questions: *"How did we get here? Who are we as a people?"* He denounced the modern distortion of history, and he was shaken by how much has been forgotten

TALCOTT TAKING A RIDE IN HIS BELOVED 1909 MODEL T

or forsaken, Sally recalls. He wanted at all costs to help people remember, she noted, and that's what much of his life was about.

In 1974, John wrote: "I believe our nation, the United States of America, is at the crossroads. ... Let us remember that by praying and fasting with God's people for our nation, we present a channel through which God can work. Fasting is a battle, both spiritually and physically, and you should be prepared to combat discouragement, doubt, hunger, and the temptation to quit too soon. 'We shall reap in due season if we faint not' (Galatians 6:8–9)."

IN 2008, FIVE YEARS BEFORE HE DIED AT THE AGE OF 105, TALCOTT WAS STILL DETERMINED TO MAKE THE JOURNEY BY BOAT TO VISIT CLARK'S ISLAND, A SMALL ISLAND IN PLYMOUTH BAY WHERE THE EXPLORING PILGRIMS TOOK SHELTER AND OBSERVED THEIR FIRST SABBATH NEAR A LARGE BOULDER KNOWN TODAY AS PULPIT ROCK. ABOVE, A 100-YEAR-OLD TALCOTT STANDS AT THE TOP PULPIT ROCK WITH DR. PAUL JEHLE AND CHARLES WOLFE

BEFORE LEAVING CLARK'S ISLAND IN 2008, TALCOTT LED A TIME OF PRAYER BY PULPIT ROCK

John was a World War II veteran, serving as an Army first lieutenant. He was 42 when he came to faith in Christ, much later in life than many converts, but even so, he perceived right away that the Lord had a clear plan for his life. Indeed, from the moment of his conversion, he was God's man through and through. As Sally recalls: "John always asked, 'What is the Lord doing?' He didn't know why he was being given a longer life [than his parents, both of whom died when they were about 70], but he didn't want to miss anything the Lord wanted him to do. He wanted to be active for God as long as possible and to bring a positive impact to each life he felt privileged to touch. He was quick to share his faith in Christ."

ENGAGE:

The nation needs people who fervently desire to be God's man or woman through and through. Ask the Lord to raise up many with such hearts, everywhere in our land.

25

MICHELLE GALLAGHER:
MONUMENTAL PRAYERS

By Dave Kubal

When I became president of IFA in 2009, I began telephoning every supporter of the ministry to thank them for their gifts. These phone calls have been some of my favorite experiences in 40 years of ministry. Connecting with intercessors, getting to know people who are called to pray for the nation, meeting new friends — I just love it.

Those connections would be enough for me, but as God tends to do, He has let me receive even greater blessings, including miraculous answers to prayer. One day I called an intercessor and learned that she had just found out she had a mass. As I prayed for her, I was filled with faith for her healing, and together we asked the Lord for complete and total healing. His answer was yes! It's amazing, but there's more: On the day she found out that the mass was no longer there, another IFA staff member "happened" to call her. We praised God together for what He did and that He gave us a front-row seat!

It is remarkable how often it happens that the seemingly random timing of an IFA call occurs right at the time of need.

IN A COLORFUL TOUR OF THIS 81-FOOT-TALL TRIBUTE TO THE PILGRIMS OF 1620, THE *FOREFATHERS MONUMENT GUIDEBOOK* EXPLORES HOW THE PILGRIMS ESTABLISHED SELF-GOVERNMENT AT PLYMOUTH COLONY AND GAVE BIRTH TO AMERICA

Over the years, as IFA has grown, this effort has continued, with the calls now being made by a team of people, not just me. One of these team callers is Tom Sampley, my father-in-law. Proceeding through his supporter list one day, Tom phoned Michelle Gallagher, of Plymouth, Massachusetts. "How can I pray for you?" Tom asked.

Many IFA supporters are hesitant about disclosing personal needs, and Michelle was no exception. But that day, she had a pressing need related to a book she had written, so she decided to share her concern. She explained to Tom that she had left her job in 2019 to produce a book on the Forefathers Monument, an 81-foot-tall monument in Plymouth built to honor the legacy of the Pilgrims. After discovering the monument in her local neighborhood, Michelle felt God's leading to create a high-quality guidebook that would explain the monument's message of faith and freedom to tourists visiting "America's Hometown." She had never written or designed a book before, but when God calls, He also equips.

THROUGH SYMBOLIC GRANITE FIGURES, MARBLE PANELS, AND LOWER RELIEFS, THE FOREFATHERS MONUMENT PAYS TRIBUTE TO THE LEGACY OF THE PILGRIMS IN THE FOUNDING OF AMERICA

Now in its third printing as a hardcover book, the *Forefathers Monument Guidebook* is impressive. In fact, Kirk Cameron, who produced and starred in the 2012 documentary *Monumental: In Search of America's National Treasure,* has personally endorsed it.

MICHELLE AND DAN GALLAGHER, FOUNDERS OF PROCLAMATION HOUSE, INC.

As a follow-up project, Michelle was further inspired to create a devotional based on the biblical principles celebrated in the Forefathers Monument. So, shortly after the *Forefathers Monument Guidebook* (available at ProclamationHouse.org) was released, she wrote another book, *Monumental Prayers,* a prayer devotional inspired by the faith and godly legacy of the Pilgrims in America. As she and Tom prayed for her concerns that morning, Michelle was deeply touched and encouraged by Tom's Spirit-led, heartfelt prayer for her book projects. Before their call ended, Michelle offered to send copies of both books to Tom in gratitude for his prayers and interest, which she did.

A few weeks later, I happened to stop by Tom's house while on a work trip. Tom showed these books to me, and I knew immediately that I had to find a way to get *Monumental Prayers* into the hands of IFA intercessors.

Several weeks later, I called Michelle and her husband, Dan. They didn't know that IFA has deep roots in Plymouth and is strongly connected to the history of the Pilgrims. I told them how IFA founder Derek Prince was invited to speak at the 350th anniversary of the *Mayflower's* landing in Plymouth. Although

ALONG WITH DEREK PRINCE (LEFT), BILLY GRAHAM (RIGHT) WAS ALSO A SPEAKER AT THE 350TH ANNIVERSARY OF THE PILGRIM'S LANDING (CENTER) IN PLYMOUTH, MASSACHUSETTS, IN 1970

THE 81-FOOT-TALL FOREFATHERS MONUMENT OVERLOOKS PLYMOUTH'S FAMOUS HARBOR

Derek had never studied the Pilgrims as a student in British schools, he was amazed at their story, which he recounted in his book, *Shaping History Through Prayer & Fasting.* That book inspired his teaching at the very conference that sparked the idea for IFA among those who became its founders.

Michelle and Dan were surprised to learn that IFA was originally incorporated as an organization in Plymouth. It remained headquartered there for years while John Talcott, a founder of the Plymouth Rock Foundation, served as president of IFA. Dan mentioned that he had known John, and he shared stories of having watched him march in Plymouth's annual Fourth of July Parade, when John was well into his late 90s. As we swapped stories of Plymouth and spoke about the people and history we hold in common, it was incredible to realize how God had connected us through Tom's "random" phone call to Michelle.

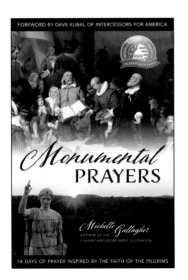

I knew this connection had been orchestrated by the Lord. I invited Michelle to create an expanded, special edition of *Monumental Prayers* to release for IFA's 50th anniversary. This partnership between IFA and Michelle and Dan's company, Proclamation House, Inc., produced *Monumental Prayers: 14 Days of Prayer Inspired by the Faith of the Pilgrims* (available from IFA).

In the book's foreword, I wrote: *"As a resident of Plymouth and one who is praying for her community, Michelle had a vision of what she could do to celebrate the Pilgrim legacy and help equip each of us to pray into the rich inheritance we have all received through them."*

Beginning with a single step of faith into the unknown, God has used Michelle's books to inspire readers with the enduring legacy of the Pilgrims — and to encourage intercessors everywhere to contend for a spiritual legacy in their own family, city, and nation.

ENGAGE:

Is there something you've never done before but which, by faith, you could trust Christ to empower you to do to advance His kingdom? Remember: He qualifies the called, rather than calling the qualified. Why not believe Him and step out?

26

NANCY RIFE: 50 YEARS OF OBEDIENCE AND ENDURANCE

By Keith Guinta

Imagine being a prayer warrior in northern Michigan in the early 1970s, during the heart of the Jesus Movement, and hearing that Derek Prince would be speaking at a conference in Fort Lauderdale, Florida. Nancy Rife and her husband, Curt, sensed that the Lord wanted them to attend this conference, advertised as being "for men called into positions of leadership and responsibility in the Body of Christ." The meeting was also intended to help attendees deal with "the problems and challenges which are unique to leadership in our day."

Nancy knew right away in her spirit that the flames of revival were going to begin burning brightly in Florida, and she was not about to miss that. "I just knew we had to go!" she explains whenever she recounts the story.

CURT AND NANCY RIFE IN 1973

So, on a frigid Michigan day in November 1973, the Rifes and an expectant band of bundled-up believers all piled into a rickety VW bus with no heat, intent on braving a 23-hour drive in the grip of the cold to attend the conference. Nancy exuberantly describes that meeting as if it were yesterday: "There were 1,000 people there! We could all feel the power and presence of God in the room. The speakers were anointed, the prayer was transcendent, and the gifts of the Spirit were flowing from the platform. In the very first meeting, there were tongues and interpretation!"

One of the men with whom Nancy and Curt had come to the conference was a train engineer from the Upper Peninsula of Michigan. Before he was saved, this man had sold drugs on the side. After he was saved, he began sharing the gospel with the people who had bought drugs from him. During this time of the Jesus Movement, these kinds of stories were not unusual.

THE VW BUS THE RIFES DROVE ON THEIR 23-HOUR JOURNEY TO ATTEND THE CONFERENCE IN FLORIDA

Another man who came with them worked at an air base in Michigan. He was delivered from demonic oppression at the conference. When they asked him about it, they found out he had not ever been saved.

IN MIAMI BEACH, A YOUNG MAN ACCEPTED CHRIST AND WAS IMMEDIATELY BAPTIZED IN THE OCEAN IN FRONT OF THE DEAUVILLE HOTEL, WHERE THE CONFERENCE WAS HELD

So he received Christ and was baptized right then on the beach in Miami, in front of the Deauville hotel.

Given that the conference speakers wanted to deal with the challenges of the day, it is perhaps no wonder that Derek Prince gathered all the leaders on the second night of the conference and urged them to do something about Roe v. Wade. That night became the beginning of IFA, and Nancy was all in. This is the eternally immutable characteristic that has sustained 50 years of ministry: a yielding to the prominence of the Holy Spirit

THE DEAUVILLE HOTEL IN MIAMI BEACH, FLORIDA, WHERE THE IDEA FOR IFA FIRST BEGAN IN 1973

to preside with power and freedom upon IFA. Said Nancy: "In 1973, when Roe v. Wade was decided, I knew that we must pray, because God would surely judge our nation harshly. And as fierce as the opposition was back in the '70s, it was nothing compared to what is happening today."

In December 2020, Nancy's dear husband died of COVID, and yet her ministry of prayer continues. She repeatedly heard the Lord tell her: "Others may do what they will, but it is imperative you raise up a house of prayer." Nancy's vision helped her start a prayer room in her home state of Michigan.

Clearly, Nancy has filled many of heaven's bowls with the incense of intercession for our country. She is a monthly guest on IFA's Headline Prayer Live webcast, and she says she is deeply grateful for how IFA's resources have informed and fueled her prayers through these many years. Yet, she believes that the greatest answers to our prayers are just ahead.

IFA CO-FOUNDER JOHN BECKETT WITH NANCY RIFE AT AN IFA EVENT

ENGAGE:

Begin praying daily that God would raise up multitudes of those who will build houses of prayer in their neighborhoods and churches — and that He would make you a house-of-prayer builder yourself.

LT. COL. OLIVER NORTH TESTIFIES BEFORE THE IRAN-CONTRA CONGRESSIONAL COMMITTEE IN 1987

27

LT. COL. OLIVER NORTH: PRAYER FREED ME

By Lt. Col. Oliver North

God has protected and blessed me all my life. But for more than 30 years, I failed to acknowledge His active, personal interest. Through all those years, He patiently coaxed me toward the pathway to true freedom (I can see that now), but I persisted in blundering down my own path in determined ignorance.

As a child growing up in the Catholic Church, I never doubted God's existence, and I learned to respect Him deeply. From a distance.

Years later, God showed me that He was closer to me than I was willing to admit. My friends and I were driving through heavy snow late at night on a weekend ski trip. It was 1964, my first year at the Naval Academy. Everyone had fallen asleep — including the driver. I jerked awake just in time to see the headlights of the oncoming truck. Then we hit. The carnage was terrible. One of my friends was killed, and the other three were badly mangled. In comparison, my injuries were relatively minimal head injuries, crushed vertebrae in my lower spine, broken nose, broken jaw, broken leg, and one damaged knee. But my surgeries and recovery kept me down for months.

I fought my way back. Sure, I gave God His credit. During my stay at the naval hospital, I made it my daily habit to wheel into the hospital chapel to pray. And God healed me so completely that four years later I won the brigade boxing championship. But my relationship with God was still one-sided — I sent up my requests, and He took care of me. I simply wasn't listening to what He was trying to tell me.

Prayer is like a two-way radio, which is designed both to transmit and receive. But my radio was stuck on "transmit." I thought, more than anything else, that my own dogged persistence had brought me back to health and allowed me to finish my academy training. I was determined to become a Marine, and I was sure no obstacle was insurmountable.

God stuck by me through my year in Vietnam, as I patrolled the so-called demilitarized zone. On several occasions, men standing right next to me were killed, while I was either untouched or back in action in very short order.

God also saved me from another kind of disaster. In my zealous commitment to the Marine Corps, I almost threw away two of His greatest gifts to me: my marriage and my family.

In the early 1970s, I found myself in Okinawa doing what I enjoyed more than anything else: training Marines. When I wrote to my wife, Betsy, that I would be missing my second Christmas in a row with her and the kids, she took longer than usual to respond. In her next letter, she wrote, "I've had enough. I want a divorce. Here's the name of my attorney."

U.S. MARINES GATHER NEAR A BUNKER FOR CHRISTMAS SERVICES

I tried to tell myself that I didn't care, that my work was the only truly important priority. But the honest part of me, the part that hurt so desperately, wouldn't buy it. The internal struggle took its toll. I ended up in the hospital, my exhausted body racked with bronchitis and my tormented spirit mired in clinical depression. I reluctantly submitted to psychiatric care and then marriage counseling, gradually recovering and ultimately reconciling with Betsy. But even through those excruciating days, I still imagined that my progress and my healing were the result of my own hard work.

One early promotion followed another, only because I was a good officer. Or so I thought. All the while, God was preparing my wake-up call.

By 1978, I had known Lt. Col. John Grinalds for about three years. He was on the fast track through the ranks. Top of his class at West Point and highly decorated from his two tours of duty in Vietnam, he had gone on to become a Rhodes scholar and a White House Fellow and to earn a Harvard MBA.

Oh, and there was one other characteristic that set Grinalds apart from the rest: He was one of those "born-again Christians." Whatever that meant. Along with all the usual training and administrative manuals on his desk, he kept a Bible. Right there in plain sight. And he read it.

Grinalds was assigned as a battalion commander to the Second Marine Division, based at Camp Lejeune, and he honored me by asking me to come along as his operations officer. I was happy to hitch my wagon to his rapidly rising star. In my new role, I was third in command, responsible for the training and preparation of a 2,000-man unit for deployment to the Mediterranean.

One morning, about two weeks before we were due to deploy, our battalion was conducting a training exercise. I had just adjusted the antenna on an armored amphibious vehicle and, spurning the ladder on the side, jumped to the ground. Big mistake.

AN AMPHIBIOUS ASSAULT VEHICLE SPLASHES OFF THE COAST OF NORTH CAROLINA DURING SHIP OPERATION TRAINING AT CAMP LEJEUNE MARINE BASE

Instant memories of the 1964 car accident flashed through my pain-racked mind. I had reinjured my back in exactly the same place. I lay writhing on the ground. I couldn't feel my legs. Lost control of my bladder.

Before a medic could arrive, John Grinalds showed up. Next thing I knew, he was putting his hands on my legs and saying, "I'm going to

Pray? I thought. I'm lying here in agony, and you want to pray!

But what I said aloud was, "Uh, Colonel, don't you think we could just do this the usual way? You know, get the helicopter, go to the hospital?"

But Grinalds ignored me. He called out: "Lord Jesus Christ, You are the Great Physician. Heal this man."

In that very instant, the pain disappeared. Soon the feeling returned to my legs. When I was ready, Grinalds helped me to my feet.

Astonished, I came out with one of the most inane utterances of my life. I said, "Thank you, sir."

At that, Grinalds grabbed me by my jacket and pulled me up to his face. "Don't thank me," he said. "Thank your Lord and Savior. He is the Great Physician. You have to turn to Him."

That incident was the two-by-four God used to break through my thick-skulled resistance. I had it in my head that freedom meant taking care of myself, forging my own path through the jungle of life's challenges. I knew that God was there to help, but I expected Him to follow my lead. What I came to realize was that He had been leading all along — and that I had not done well at following. I had been placing my faith in myself, yet He had been telling me over and over: "You'll only be truly free when you know and trust Me."

This realization profoundly humbled me. During the six months of our Mediterranean deployment, I participated in Bible studies with Grinalds and managed to read the Bible

cover to cover. I learned that I had known a lot about God, but I had not known Him personally. I had sent a lot of orders in His direction, and He had even deigned to "obey" some of them. But I had been living in servitude to self; now, I was discovering true freedom, living as I was designed to live: in relationship with God.

I had grown up believing in the vending-machine concept of prayer: You put in your quarter, and you get back your selection, all neatly wrapped and sealed. But now, I've come to understand that prayer is a freely

LT. COL. NORTH WITH PRESIDENT RONALD REAGAN AT THE WHITE HOUSE IN 1982

flowing, two-way conversation with a Person. In fact, prayer doesn't even require words. Prayer at its best involves intimate, heart-to-heart communion with God, with or without words.

OLIVER AND BETSY NORTH IN 2006

Prayer is the voice of faith — and the pathway to true freedom. True freedom is the opposite of arrogant self-determination. It is submission to God's will. When I enthrone my own will and pursue my own "best," I severely limit myself. When I obey God, I open myself to His unlimited blessing. Jesus Himself said that if you obey His teachings, "you will know the truth, and the truth will set you free" (John 8:32).

LT. COL. NORTH AS A FOX NEWS REPORTER IN 2012, INTERVIEWING MARINE CAPT. KEVIN T. SMALLEY AT CAMP BASTION IN AFGHANISTAN

How can you learn to trust God enough to submit yourself to His will? Only by growing to know Him. Only by living life in conversation with Him. Only through a lifestyle of prayer. Your Creator and Lord wants to relate to you as Friend and Father. He made you for one primary purpose: to live in an intimate relationship with Him. When you fulfill that purpose, you find true freedom.

ENGAGE:

The next time you pray with someone who does not know Jesus Christ, whether for their healing or for any other need, remind that person afterward that he or she needs Him personally, for salvation and for the blessings of peace — both in this life and the next.

PASTOR ANDREW BRUNSON AND HIS WIFE, NORINE, PREPARE TO LEAVE TURKEY SHORTLY AFTER HIS RELEASE

28

ANDREW BRUNSON: MISSIONARY DELIVERED FROM PRISON

By Judy McDonough

In 2016, a failed coup in Turkey incited President Recep Tayyip Erdogan to arrest hundreds of thousands of Turkish residents, whom he accused of terrorism. Among those arrested were Pastor Andrew Brunson and his wife, Norine. They had led a church for 25 years in that country, serving mostly Syrian refugees. The Brunsons had nothing to do with terrorism, the coup, or any political disputes in Turkey. Norine was released quickly, but Pastor Brunson was kept in custody. "Somebody decided to hold us, and I think that was to intimidate other missionaries, so they would self-deport," Pastor Brunson said. "At some point, I became, obviously, a use for leverage to try to gain concessions from the U.S. There is a human story and the God story. What Erdogan was doing, I was his hostage, but when God had completed what He wanted through my imprisonment, then He caused my release."

That powerful statement of faith was made in an interview with PBS NewsHour after the publication of his book, *God's Hostage: A True Story of Persecution, Imprisonment, and Perseverance,* in 2019. This perspective is where God brought him, though he did suffer greatly during his two years of imprisonment.

As a foreign missionary in Turkey, Pastor Brunson had given much thought to the possibility of imprisonment and to how he would respond if he were detained. He anticipated that he would be praising God and experiencing spiritual highs. "Many of the biographies I have read of who I would call Christian heroes, my heroes, they show very strong people," Pastor Brunson said. "And I expected that, when I was suffering, I would

FROM LEFT: TRACEY DEBLANK, JUDY MCDONOUGH, ANDREW BRUNSON, AND KRIS KUBAL AT AN IFA EVENT

also have that strength. And instead, I felt very broken and weak." He clung to his faith, but he struggled. He would press through to accept his situation, and then something worse would happen, over and over.

At a National Day of Prayer event shortly after Pastor Brunson's release, IFA staff had the opportunity to meet him and to hear him tell his story. His face and body showed signs of the impact of his ordeal, yet he also demonstrated profound wisdom and fortitude. Norine stood by his side, exuding strength and resolve. It was easy to imagine how much he had missed her and her support during that entire time when she had remained such a tireless advocate for his release.

A U.S. CONSULATE OFFICIAL ESCORTS NORINE BRUNSON TO HER HUSBAND'S COURT HEARING IN IZMIR, TURKEY, ON OCT. 12, 2018

Pastor Brunson emphasized his dependence on the prayers of Christians in America and around the world. During the imprisonment, Norine was permitted to visit her husband once each week. They would speak together on a phone, with a thick glass separating them. The first question he would ask her, week after week, was: "Are people still praying for me?" He said he knew that people tend to move on to the next crisis, and he was worried about when Christians would move on from him, to pray for someone else.

ANDREW BRUNSON BECAME A PAWN IN TURKISH PRESIDENT ERDOĞAN'S ATTEMPTS TO CRUSH DISSENT FOLLOWING A FAILED COUP

At the prayer event, the pastor was visibly moved when most of the crowd of several hundred raised their hands upon being asked: "Have you prayed for Andrew?"

The Trump administration and a bipartisan group of lawmakers fought for Pastor Brunson's release, which finally came at a trial in July 2018. Though it was an official trial, this was never a court issue, so justice was not involved. President Erdogan made all the decisions regarding

A CONVOY CARRYING RELEASED PASTOR ANDREW BRUNSON LEAVES THE ALIAGA PRISON COURT AFTER HIS HEARING ON OCT. 12, 2018, IN IZMIR, TURKEY

Pastor Brunson. He was found guilty but received a suspended sentence and his travel ban was lifted. "And that basically means, leave as soon as you can," Pastor Brunson said. "So it was such a roller coaster to go from being convicted of terror, thinking I am going back to prison, then rushing to the airport to get on an Air Force plane and leave Turkish airspace as soon as possible, in case they change their mind. So within 24 hours, I go from being convicted of terror to visiting the White House."

"Right now the whole world is a fan of yours, the whole world is a fan," President Trump told Pastor Brunson. "It's a great honor to have you back home." And how did the pastor respond? He asked if he could pray for President Trump.

ANDREW BRUNSON, HIS FAMILY, AND ACLJ ATTORNEY CECE HEIL (RIGHT) WITH PRESIDENT TRUMP IN THE OVAL OFFICE

At the time, IFA asked one of Pastor Brunson's attorneys if she could share anything about how prayer was answered in his release. That attorney was CeCe Heil, senior counsel at the American Center for Law and Justice. Here is what she said:

"As an international human-rights attorney with the American Center for Law and Justice, I'll be the first to acknowledge that prayer changes everything. I can't guarantee that any certain outcome will be obtained, of course, but I can guarantee that hearts will be touched, evil will be thwarted, and God will be glorified. This can definitely be seen in the case of our client Pastor Brunson, who was wrongfully arrested and imprisoned in Turkey simply for living out his Christian faith. During his two years in prison, he suffered times of frustration, discouragement, and hopelessness. But while we assisted with his trial in Turkey and worked with the State Department, Congress, President Trump, Vice President Pence, and various international bodies, we never lost sight of this: It is our Lord Jesus who turns the heart of kings, gives hope to the hopeless, makes possible the impossible, and sets the captives free—figuratively and literally.

"I cannot share details of the legal and political obstacles we encountered in the Brunson case, but I'm convinced that it was only through the prayers of God's people the world over that those obstacles were overcome. Pastor Brunson has repeatedly said himself that it was those very prayers that got him through his ordeal.

"Perhaps we all hope we'll be strong if we're ever imprisoned for our faith, but we can't really have any idea until we're actually faced with that trial. We may question why we're suffering for simply being obedient to God, or wonder whether we've done something wrong, all while waiting desperately for God to intervene on our behalf. And these may in fact be questions we struggle with daily, even if we're not sitting in a prison. I think this is why intercessory prayer is so vitally important, and it's also why the epistle of James not only encourages us to pray for each other, but also reminds us that those prayers are powerful and effective. Still, there will be times when someone may feel overwhelmed or may be too discouraged to pray, as Paul himself experienced and wrote about in 2 Corinthians 1. It is in those very times that God will use the prayers of many to bring about His deliverance.

"Some may think the days of Christian persecution are past, but I assure you that they're not. The ACLJ is constantly addressing religious persecution all over the world. There are countless Christians who face death, torture, and imprisonment for their faith every day. Whether it is the Christian genocide at the hands of ISIS in Iraq and Syria, the push for forced atheism in China, the horrible atrocities against Christians in Nigeria, or the constant fear that Christians face

TOP (L-R): CHRISTIANS RISK THEIR LIVES BY MEETING IN A SECRET HOME CHURCH IN CHINA; FANA TESEMA WEEPS DURING A DEMONSTRATION ON CAPITOL HILL TO BRING AWARENESS TO GENOCIDE AGAINST ETHNIC AMHARA AND ORTHODOX CHRISTIANS IN ETHIOPIA; BOTTOM: A CHURCH BURNED BY ISLAMIC STATE MILITANTS IN KARAMLES, A CHRISTIAN TOWN IN IRAQ

in Pakistan — and those are just a few examples — I am certain there are many brothers and sisters in Christ who are discouraged and overwhelmed, and who would love for others to be praying for their deliverance."

ENGAGE:

Set aside some time to pray specifically for Christ's persecuted and imprisoned saints around the world — and even here in America. Pray too that believers may be encouraged and prepared for any future trials.

PROLOGUE:
YOUR STORY IN *GOD'S* STORY

Many of those who play a role in changing the shape of history have little awareness of their impact at the time they are doing so. As with a composer who toils through the writing of an epic symphony, the divine orchestration is not fully appreciated until future generations behold the results of the score's progression toward perfection.

Such is the case with the overturning of Roe v. Wade. IFA was established in 1973 to catalyze and organize prayer for the United States of America. That was the very year the Supreme Court legalized abortion through the Roe decision. For nearly 50 years since, as both the steadfast opposition and the horrifying body count have continued to increase, IFA has faithfully led a national movement of prayer and action to save the lives of babies, helped support the mothers, and labored tirelessly to see the court's unconstitutional ruling overturned.

From IFA's inception, there was a consensus among the ministry's founders that the sanctity of human life would remain a top priority for intercession. Along with devoted prayer and fasting, IFA developed teachings, seminars, publications, and studies to help educate and inform people about the sanctity of life and to promote a spiritual awakening.

IFA has understood from the very beginning that only a revival inspired by the Holy Spirit can transform hearts, save lives, and change the course of our nation.

Another foundational IFA tenet has been the commitment to pray fervently for our government leaders. Consider the innumerable prayers that brought about the appointments of Supreme Court Justices Neil Gorsuch, Brett Kavanaugh, and Amy Coney Barrett. On June 24, 2022, less than two years after Justice Barrett's appointment, the court ruled 5-4 that Roe v. Wade was unconstitutional, and thus sent the issue of abortion back to the states.

Can you hear a symphonic crescendo of thundering tympani and clashing cymbals, bursting forth in exultation? As we rejoice and praise God that this righteous ruling has finally been handed down, however, we dare not put down our instruments just yet, because the musical score is far from finished.

It is estimated that over 64 million babies have been murdered since Roe v. Wade. That translates to a ghastly average of over 3,500 abortions per day. So, as the rulings on abortion now return to the jurisdiction of the states, we must realize that our call to intercession is no less weighty today than it was 50 years ago. As Derek Prince wrote in the first IFA newsletter: "Intercession is one of the most profound and powerful ministries available to a Christian. To 'intercede' means literally 'to come in between.'"

May we come in between the plague of evil and injustice in our land and the looming wrath of God as we call for repentance and revival in this nation. And may we all continue playing our part in the Father's great symphony as it resounds beyond the confines of time and space. Our intercessory prayers today, rising along with the very same "incense" the IFA founders offered up in 1973, will continue to have great impact until Christ is revealed here again.

ENGAGE:

Take your place upon the wall. Stand in the gap. Plead for repentance and revival in our nation, your state, and your community.

APPENDIX:
THE STORY OF
INTERCESSORS FOR AMERICA

The "Intercessors for" networks got their start in 1969, when European Youth for Christ leader the Rev. Denis Clark and others felt prompted to set aside some hours on New Year's Day to wait upon the Lord. They earnestly sought God concerning the condition of Britain and the world. Out of that time together, these seekers concluded that they should look for Christians who could volunteer to cover every hour during each week to pray for their nation. Doing this would require 168 people, but 200 volunteered to pray for an hour each week — though there were some gaps for the night hours.

And so Intercessors for Britain (IFB) was born. As Clark evangelized and taught throughout Europe and the British Empire, he called for intercessory prayer and fasting for all nations. He and IFB became the impetus and pattern for many similar works. Though some emerged quite independently of Clark's initiative, sixteen 'IF' networks were established between 1971 and Clark's death in 1981, including IFA.

Eventually, IF leadership from the U.S., Europe, Israel, Africa, and other regions and nations helped establish more than 40 IF networks worldwide. After a divine meeting in 2020, IFA helped form the newest IF network: Intercessors for Ukraine, which launched its ministry just months before the Russian invasion catalyzed prayer in that nation. This network was divinely positioned by God to serve a nation in crisis.

Intercessors for Ukraine, Britain, Israel, and Nigeria continue to function. Others, as in Canada and Mexico, have merged into newer national prayer networks.

FROM LEFT: GUY AND KATHY KUMP, WENDY AND JOEL BECKETT, BETH CLARK, SALLY AND JAY FESPERMAN, AND DENIS CLARK

Begun in Grace by Providence

The story of the beginning of IFA is a testimony to God's grace. Two conference speakers who had never met each other spoke by phone some weeks before a 1973 conference in order to discuss possible topics. One speaker, Derek Prince, had recently published a book on the theme of praying for governments and their leaders, entitled *Shaping History Through Prayer & Fasting.*

This book "just happened" to be at the bedside of the other speaker, Ern Baxter, where it was next up to be read. Baxter pastored a large church in Vancouver, British Columbia, and had just become familiar with the intercessors movement in Britain. So impressed were the leaders of the Vancouver church that they decided to form Intercessors for Canada.

Meanwhile, the Holy Spirit was prompting people to attend what was to become a historic conference. Interestingly, although it was a men's conference, Nancy Rife, of Michigan, sensed the Lord's leading for her to join her husband in attending (see Chapter 26), as did Sally Fesperman, of North Carolina (see Chapter 24). Though their husbands have since passed on, both ladies are still part of IFA's ministry today, 50 years later.

IFA PRES./CEO DAVE KUBAL, AND WIFE KRIS, IFA CHIEF PROGRAM OFFICER

Prince and Baxter agreed that it was the Lord's heart that they should address the topic of prayer for the nations and their governments. At the time of this conference, the nation was in crisis. Political corruption; war; an energy crisis; unjust and unbiblical laws; abortion; a growing tolerance of drug use and sexual immorality; and other challenges were changing the way Americans lived and thought. Through the messages at that four-day conference in South Florida, the Lord stirred the hearts of many hundreds of believers about the importance of interceding for America.

Toward the close of the conference, on Nov. 24, 1973, Prince challenged the attendees to find a way to sustain the momentum, building a crescendo of prayer that would last at least through America's bicentennial, in 1976. Many volunteered, and an initial steering committee was formed to guide and guard this vision. That group of eight men, under the leadership of John Talcott, then laid the groundwork to begin the operation of IFA. The committee members were: Baxter, Prince, Talcott, John Beckett, Warren Black, Jay Fesperman, George Gillies, and John Heard.

Since 1973, IFA has informed, connected, and mobilized a growing number of people praying and fasting for the nation. For decades, God has inspired us to pray in accordance with His will, and He has faithfully answered our prayers. Find out more at IFApray.org.

CONTRIBUTORS

Intercessors for America has been telling the story of God's invitation to shape history through prayer and fasting since the ministry's beginnings. IFA intercessors know from personal experience that God moves His people to pray in accordance with His will so that He can answer their prayers. IFA stories, collected and told over 50 years, inspired this book.

This list of contributors honors the many who have been part of telling God's story and how our stories show up in His story. Despite our best efforts, this list may very well be incomplete and may omit the names of IFA staff members whose work was anonymous.

WANDA ALGER served as a writer and field correspondent with IFA for many years and has written for *Charisma,* The Elijah List, Spirit Fuel, and *The Christian Post.* She is an author of numerous books, including *Moving from Sword to Scepter: Ruling Through Prayer as the Ekklesia of God.* Follow her at WandaAlger.me.

NICOLE ARNOLDBIK is a writer and editor for IFA. She studied print media communications at Moody Bible Institute and Old Testament and semitics at Talbot School of Theology. She is an explorer at heart, having lived in five U.S. states (and on a Lakota Sioux Reservation), canoed along large chunks of the Lewis and Clark National Historic Trail, and taken as many U.S. road trips as time and gas would allow.

JOHN D. BECKETT co-founded IFA and has been an integral part of the organization for 50 years, serving as president, chairman of the board, and, most recently, a board member. He is also chairman of the R.W. Beckett Corporation, in northeast Ohio, a worldwide leader in engineered components for residential and commercial heating. His two books, *Loving Monday* (1998) and *Mastering Monday* (2006), focus on the integration of faith and work (www.beckettpress.com). He has lived many of the stories he writes about.

GARY BERGEL contributed to IFA from the very beginning, by assisting the Talcotts with his graphics and formatting skills, through his research and writing, and by his leadership — from the time IFA relocated to the Washington, D.C., area in June, 1985, until his retirement in 2009. His historical writing was invaluable in the selection and retelling of these stories.

JILL CATALDO met Jesus through the ministry of Young Life, an outreach to high school students. She later served on the Young Life staff for some 20 years with her husband, Luis. Jill and Luis have been in the prayer movement working with Passion, The International House of Prayer in Kansas City, The Call, The Response, The Cedars/National Prayer Breakfast, American Renewal Project, and The Strategic Resource Group. Jill has been an intercessor for various governmental leaders in the United States. She is currently an IFA researcher and has contributed key details for these historic stories.

MICHELLE GALLAGHER helped develop the vision for this book and then went on to design and publish it. She is the author of the *Forefathers Monument Guidebook* and *Monumental Prayers: 14 Days of Prayer Inspired by the Faith of the Pilgrims*. Both projects were published through Proclamation House, Inc., a nonprofit organization Michelle and her husband, Dan, established to create quality books that herald faith and freedom to the generations (www.ProclamationHouse.org).

KEITH GUINTA is an IFA contributing writer and a prayer leader on IFA's Headline Prayer Live. He also blogs at winepatch.org. Keith's writing pours out from years of walking in step with the Spirit.

DAVE KUBAL has been president and CEO of IFA since 2008, and he is the author of three books: *Inspired Prayers; Inspired People*; and *Fasting.* As a nationally recognized faith leader, Dave serves on the National Faith Advisory Board and the National Day of Prayer Task Force. From the start of his leadership, Dave has emphasized the value of the intercessor as a person, as well as the need to connect each intercessor to the unfolding news, which is in fact history in the making. IFA has grown exponentially under his leadership.

MACKENZIE KUBAL is IFA's member-relations assistant. This book would not have existed without her careful transcribing of historical documents and her openness to share about the stories that moved her.

ARLYN LAWRENCE is a writer, editor, and speaker with a passion for prayer and equipping the Body of Christ. She is the founder of Inspira Literary Solutions, and the co-author of several books, including *Prayer-Saturated Kids* with Cheryl Sacks (NavPress/Tyndale). She lives with her husband in Gig Harbor, Washington.

JUDY MCDONOUGH is the lead editor of *Inspired Stories,* IFA's communications director, and co-author of *Inspired People.* In her career as a lawyer, Judy worked as general counsel for Care Net, a national network of crisis-pregnancy centers. After spending two decades as an at-home mother, Bible study leader, non-profit board member and volunteer, Judy joined IFA in 2017 as a writer and editor. In 2018, Judy assumed the role of communications director. She oversees a team of fifteen dedicated content producers who create digital and print content that captures the spiritual realities of America's rapidly-changing news and hosts IFA's weekly webcast, *Headline Prayer Live.* She is passionate about the power of prayer to impact our nation and transform lives for Jesus.

AARON MERCER is a gifted IFA contributing writer with over two decades of experience in ministry communications and the public-policy arena of Washington, D.C.

DAVID ORTIZ is an anointed wordsmith who helped craft the vision for this volume before carefully editing, proofreading, and poring over every word. He graduated summa cum laude from the City University of New York, has written and edited for numerous magazines, and has been a guest lecturer for the World Journalism Institute. As staff editor, David brings both spiritual depth and three decades of professional writing and editing experience to IFA's content team.

SUNI PIPER served as an IFA contributing writer and webcast prayer leader. As a passionate intercessor for this nation and for the Church, she is determined and surrendered to be a voice of truth and encouragement to Christian believers everywhere.

GLORIA ROBLES is one of IFA's most popular contributing writers. She combines humility, discernment, and clear communication in a way that touches readers' hearts.

KAREN VERCRUSE was an IFA intercessor and contributing writer. She served on the Butte County Board of Supervisors, in California, and was only the fourth woman ever to hold that position. She was passionate about her city and also about helping intercessors realize the power of prayer to transform communities. She went home to the Lord in January 2023.

BETSY WEST is an IFA writer and leads IFA's Pennsylvania state prayer group with her husband, Bill. The Wests are also frequent hosts and guests of the IFA webcasts. Betsy's deep, unshakeable faith is an inspiration to all who know her. She is truly a shepherd after God's own heart.

CREDITS

CHAPTER 1. THE MOST PRAYED-FOR PERSON IN AMERICA
Photo credits: Becky Currie, Becky Currie private collection; premature baby, Getty Images/andresr; Supreme Court demonstration, Getty Images/Brandon Bell/staff; IFA archives.

CHAPTER 2. HOW THE BERLIN WALL *REALLY* CAME DOWN
Originally published at IFApray.org, October 2022.
Photo credits: Reagan White House photo collection: 1981–1989, public domain, via Wikimedia Commons; closed Brandenburg Gate, Getty Images/Sparwasser; peace sign through Berlin Wall, Getty Images/FrankvandenBergh; candlelight vigil, Getty Images/LewisTsePuiLung; Russian tank, Getty Images/Vyacheslav Argenberg; celebration upon the Berlin Wall, Getty Images/Steve Eason/Stringer.

CHAPTER 3. 'SUDDENLY' IN THE SOVIET UNION
From articles originally published by IFA, April 1990 and January 1994.
Photo credits: The Baltic Way, in Moteris magazine © L. Vasauskas/CC-BY-SA-4.0 — https://commons.wikimedia.org/wiki/File:Baltic_Way_in_Moteris_magazine.jpeg; John and Wendy Beckett, Beckett family private collection; Izmailovo Hotel, by Artem Svetlov, from Moscow, Russia/CC BY 2.0/https://creativecommons.org/licenses/by/2.0/ https://commons.wikimedia.org/wiki/File:Izmailovo_hotel_complex_drone_(36025865024).jpg; Reagan greets boy, Getty Images/The White House/Handout; view of the Kremlin, Getty Images/Soltan Frédéric.

CHAPTER 4. TERRORIST PLANS THWARTED
From an article originally published by IFA, September 1976.
Photo credits: marching bands in front of the Capitol, Getty Images, Pictorial Parade/staff; President and First Lady Ford watching fireworks from the White House balcony, Wikimedia Commons, public domain; Dr. James Rhoads cutting a giant birthday cake, Getty Images/Pictorial Parade/staff; the Magna Carta presented to the U.S. by the House of Lords, Getty Images/Pictorial Parade/staff.

CHAPTER 5. THE TIMELY BIRTH OF INTERCESSORS FOR UKRAINE
Originally published by IFA, May 2022.
Photo credits: U.S.-Ukrainian flags, Getty Images/Sckrepka; President Trump at the National Day of Prayer, the White House, from Washington, D.C., public domain, via Wikimedia Commons; volunteers pack meals for Ukraine, IFA archives; gospel booklets, IFA archives; Ukrainian billboard, IFA archives; paratroopers, Getty Images/Handout; soldier praying, Getty Images/Jason Hohnberger; Intercessors for Ukraine collage, IFA archives.

CHAPTER 6. *SAVING AZIZ*— AND MANY OTHERS
Originally published by IFA, March 2023.
Photo credits: U.S. soldiers guard Kabul airport, Sgt. Isaiah Campbell, public domain, via Wikimedia Commons; Tommy Waller, IFA collection; troops stand guard in Afghanistan, Getty Images/Handout/Handout; Chad Robichaux, courtesy of Mighty Oaks Foundation; *Saving Aziz* book cover, courtesy of Mighty Oaks Foundation; Aziz and family, courtesy of Mighty Oaks Foundation; Panj River between Tajikistan and Afghanistan, Getty Images/Tuul and Bruno Morandi.

CHAPTER 7. ASSASSINATION PLAN SUPERNATURALLY STOPPED
Originally published at IFApray.org, June 2022.
Photo credits: praying at the Supreme Court, Getty Images/Drew Angerer/staff; protests at the Supreme Court, Getty Images/Drew Angerer/staff; the post-Roe generation, Getty Images/Anna Rose Layden/Stringer; demonstration at Justice Kavanaugh's home, Getty Images/Bonnie Cash/Stringer; "Resign Kavanaugh" written in chalk on the pavement, Getty

Images/Alex Wong/staff; Supreme Court justices, Getty Images/Pool/Pool; Glock with ammo, Getty Images/Steve Dunning; guards at Justice Kavanaugh's home, Getty Images/Bonnie Cash/Stringer; suspect arrested, Getty Images/SimonSkafar; contemplation of Justice statue, Getty Images/photo by Robert Mooney; Authority of Law statue, Getty Images/baumsaway.

CHAPTER 8. A HOMETOWN VICTORY
Originally published by IFA, May 1983.
Photo credits: autumn leaves, Getty Images/Ali Majdfar; John and Wendy Beckett, Beckett family private collection; professional building, Getty Images/CynthiaAnnF; 1983 pro-life billboard, Elyria ponders abortion rules, signed petitions, supporter weeps, and unanimous vote, all reproduced from Intercessors for America newsletter, May 1, 1983, vol. 10, No. 5.

CHAPTER 9. MISSISSIPPI *TURNING*
Originally published by IFA, May 2015.
Photo credits: KKK burning cross, Getty Images/William Campbell/contributor; *Mississippi Burning* movie set, Getty Images/Robert R. McElroy/contributor; Neshoba County Courthouse — CapCase, CC BY 2.0 https://creativecommons.org/licenses/by/2.0, via Wikimedia Commons; Dr. Martin Luther King Jr., Getty Images/Bettmann/contributor; bodies recovered, Getty Images/Pool/Pool; burned-out car, Getty Images/Pool/Pool; Freedom Summer Murders sign, Getty Images/Marianne Todd/Stringer; memorial at Mt. Nemo Missionary Baptist Church, Getty Images/Marianne Todd/Stringer; Rita Schwerner lights a candle at a memorial service, Getty Images/Marianne Todd/Stringer; circle gathering after service, Getty Images/Marianne Todd/Stringer; Edgar Killen waves outside the courtroom in 1966, Getty Images/Bettmann/contributor; three civil-rights workers killed, Getty Images/Underwood Archives/contributor; people gather outside the courthouse, Getty Images/Marianne Todd/Stringer; Edgar Killen in 1964, Getty Images/Pool/Pool; Edgar Killen in 2005, Getty Images/Pool/Pool; Chaney family at the casket of James Chaney, Getty Images/Bettmann/contributor; Ben Chaney in 2005, Getty Images/Marianne Todd/Stringer.

CHAPTER 10. GOD'S STRATEGY FOR SATANCON
Originally published by IFA, April 2023.
Photo credits: attendee at SatanCon, Getty Images/Spencer Platt/staff; Suzie and Lynne MacAskill, IFA archives; IFA website, IFA archives; collage of intercessors and symbolic prayer items at the hotel, courtesy of Marylou Francisco; Be Not Afraid, pentagram, "Hail Satan" fan with Jesus doll, The Little Black Church, "unbaptism" ceremony, Christians kneel to pray in Boston, all Getty Images/Spencer Platt/staff.

CHAPTER 11. A FIRST FRIDAY MIRACLE
Photo credits: flag on porch of a home, Getty Images/Traveler1116; group praying in front of a cross, Getty Images/Cat Lane; Civil War ruins in Richmond, the War Department, the office of the chief signal officer, public domain, via Wikimedia Commons; modern view of state Capitol building, in Richmond, Getty Images/Sky Noir Photography by Bill Dickinson; holding hands, Getty Images/Eclipse_images; blurry church interior, Getty Images/Christin Lola; Richmond skyline, Getty Images/Joe Daniel Price.

CHAPTER 12. COMPLAINING DOESN'T BRING CHANGE – *PRAYER* DOES
Originally published by IFA, October 2014.
Photo credits: frat-party drinking, Getty Images/Chuck Savage; Chico State, Kendall Hall, in March 2020, Frank Schulenburg, CC BY-SA 4.0 https://creativecommons.org/licenses/by-sa/4.0, via Wikimedia Commons; Senator Theatre Building, Chico, in the fall of 2020 (cropped), Frank Schulenburg, CC BY-SA 4.0 https://creativecommons.org/licenses/by-sa/4.0, via Wikimedia Commons; Chico City Plaza, Panoramio — MARELBU, CC BY 3.0 https://creativecommons.org/licenses/by/3.0, via Wikimedia Commons; hands raised, Getty Images/Kativ; campus of Chico State, Daderot, CC0, via Wikimedia Commons; Trinity bell tower, Daderot, CC0, via Wikimedia Commons; City Council meeting, Getty Images/Owen Franken.

CHAPTER 13. FROM 'DEPRESSED CITY USA' TO CITY OF HOPE
Originally published in Prayer Connect magazine, vol. 1, No. 1. Used with permission of Arlyn Lawrence and Church Prayer Leaders Network.
Photo credits: No Trespassing, Getty Images/Scott Olson/staff; drug deal, Getty Images/Luka Lajst; blurred interior of a church, Getty Images/WDnet; view of Cumberland Gap, Getty Images/JillLang; Jesus Is Lord of Clay County sign, Getty Images/LordHenriVoton; woman contemplating, Getty Images/Carlos Ciudad Photos; FBI agent, Getty Images/Nes; judge's gavel, Getty Images/Chris Ryan; film director, Getty Images/Vuk Ostojic; Bible, Getty Images/Art Plus; cross in a church lobby, Getty Images/Cosminxp Cosmin; mist over Kentucky hills, Getty Images/Cris Ritchie Photo.

CHAPTER 14. D.C. CRIME RATE PLUMMETS
Originally published by IFA, July 2000.
Photo credits: The Capitol at sunset, Getty Images/Doug Armand; The Washington Monument, Getty Images/Prasit; a man in handcuffs, Getty Images/Jub Rubjob; traffic in front of the Capitol, Getty Images/Allan Baxter; D.C. police, Getty Images/Drew Angerer/staff; Tidal Basin at night, Getty Images/Tanarch.

CHAPTER 15. PRAYER AND THE BELTWAY SNIPERS
Truck driver Ron Lantz was widely credited with helping police capture the serial killers known as the Beltway snipers. Originally published by IFA, December 2003. Reprinted with permission, Guideposts, September 2003.
Photo credits: A truck driving through hills; Getty Images/Jetta Productions Inc; blurred image of a nurse walking, Getty Images/OZANKUTSAL; stained-glass window in a church, Getty Images/DarcyMaulsby; a note left from the snipers, Getty Images/Pool/Pool; a trucker on CB, Getty Images/welcomia; truck convoy, Getty Images/ianmcdonnell; a shooter-in-trunk police video demonstration, Getty Images/Pool/Pool; map of the locations of the Beltway sniper attacks, User:Tom, CC BY-SA 3.0 http://creativecommons.org/licenses/by-sa/3.0, via Wikimedia Commons; FBI agents investigating D.C. sniper crime scene, FBI/public domain, via Wikimedia Commons; a filled-up truck stop, Getty Images/Miguel Perfectti; license plate, FBI/public domain, via Wikimedia Commons; snipers' blue Chevrolet Caprice after capture, Getty Images/Pool/Pool; truck headlights, Getty Images/Douglas Sacha; police-car lights, Getty Images/MattGush; under arrest, Getty Images/kali9; Ron Lantz speaking to reporters, Getty Images/Mike Simons/Stringer; John Allen Muhammad, Getty Images/Pool/Pool; Lee Boyd Malvo, Getty Images/Mark Wilson/staff; sniper caught, Getty Images/Mario Tama/staff.

CHAPTER 16. PARENTS AND A SCHOOL REVOLUTION
From articles published by IFA, 2020–2023.
Photo credits: I Am Not an Oppressor sign, Getty Images/Andrew Caballero-Reynolds/contributor; school friends, Getty Images/Maskot; Loudoun County school protest, IFA collection; Nancy Huff, Huff private family collection; We Don't Co-Parent w/the Govt sign, Getty Images/Octavio Jones/Stringer; parent with child speaks at a public forum, Getty Images/Octavio Jones/Stringer; mother with a child doing homework on a laptop, Getty Images/FG Trade; family walking with flags, Getty Images/Jon Cherry/Stringer.

CHAPTER 17. MARK LEE DICKSON: SANCTUARY CITIES FOR THE UNBORN
Originally published by IFA, May 2021.
Photo credits: Abortion Stops a Beating Heart bumper sticker, Getty Images/Jon Cherry/Stringer; Mark Lee Dickson with headline paper, courtesy of www.markleedickson.com; Planned Parenthood building, Getty Images/Welles Enterprises; baby's feet, Getty Images/guruXOOX.

CHAPTER 18. RESCUING THE PERISHING
Originally published by IFA, July 2021.
Photo credits: Gate at Dachau, Getty Images/Alexeys; Mark Lee Dickson, Kim Primavera, and other leaders, Primavera signing sanctuary-city law, courtesy of Kim Primavera; woman

praying, Getty Images/PeteWill.

CHAPTER 19. REPENTANCE HEALS THE LAND
Originally published by IFA, July 2021.
Photo credits: aerial view of lands irrigated from the Ogallala Aquifer, Getty Images/NNehring; map of water-level changes in the High Plains/Ogallala Aquifer, Kbh3rd, CC BY-SA 3.0 https://creativecommons.org/licenses/by-sa/3.0, via Wikimedia Commons; Gov. Sam Brownback of Kansas makes remarks at a groundbreaking ceremony at McConnell Air Force Base, Kansas City District U.S. Army Corps of Engineers, CC BY 2.0 https://creativecommons.org/licenses/by/2.0, via Wikimedia Commons; official portrait of Sam Brownback as a U.S. senator for Kansas, United States Congress, public domain, via Wikimedia Commons; Potawatomi Trail of Death sign near Argos, Indiana, Chris Light, CC BY-SA 4.0 https://creativecommons.org/licenses/by-sa/4.0, via Wikimedia Commons; view of a sunset over a wheat field in Kansas, Getty Images/Audrey Burnett/500px; Ambassador Brownback delivers remarks to the media, U.S. State Department, public domain, via Wikimedia Commons; IFA's Dave Kubal honors Sam Brownback, IFA archives; Christian leaders gather at the Congressional Cemetery for prayer in 2021, IFA archives.

CHAPTER 20. SHERRIE MOORE: FOLLOWING THE LAMB
Originally published by IFA, November 2015.
Photo credits: Christian markings over Egyptian Temple carvings, courtesy of Judy McDonough; Sherrie and Matthew Moore, Early Citywide Gatherings, RIHOP prayer room, Pastor Agayby, 'Blessed Be Egypt' sign in church, Jewels of the Nile micro-businesses, Sherrie Moore ministering in Minya, Egypt, MAPS Global prayer room, Sherrie and Matthew Moore, courtesy of Sherrie Moore.

CHAPTER 21. BIBLES IN SCHOOLS
Originally published by IFA, September 2022.
Photo credits: boy with Spanish Bible, Hannah Sailsbury with students holding Bibles, young girl checks Bible out of the library, Bible on student's desk, boy reading a Bible in a story group, school students holding Bibles, all courtesy of Bibles in Schools; *The Action Storybook Bible* cover, courtesy of David C. Cook Publishers; smiling student at the school library, Getty Images/Olga Mosman.

CHAPTER 22. DEREK PRINCE: 'TEACHER OF THE SCRIPTURES'
From many articles published by IFA over 50 years.
Photo credits: King's College, Getty Images/Anna Denisova; Derek Prince at Trinity Church, Derek Prince quote and picture, courtesy of Derek Prince Ministries; Mayflower II, Getty Images/OlegAlbinsky; Shaping History Through Prayer and Fasting book covers, 1973, 2023, courtesy of Derek Prince Ministries and IFA; IFA founding members' signatures, courtesy of John D. Beckett; the grave of Derek Prince — RonAlmog from Israel (ישראלי), CC BY 2.0 https://creativecommons.org/licenses/by/2.0, via Wikimedia Commons; IFA group in Washington, D.C., IFA archives.

CHAPTER 23. BETSY WEST: DISCOVERING BURIED TREASURE
Photo credits: Western Pennsylvania landscape, Getty Images/ZRPhoto; Betsy and Bill West, IFA archives; file records, Getty Images/Ezza116; Pennsylvania map, Getty Images/Ideabug; light through trees, Getty Images/Brian Caissie; candle on Bible, Getty Images/Alan M. Barr; Washington, Pennsylvania, panorama, Pastor Joe Jeffreys, both Best Ward private collection.

CHAPTER 24. JOHN TALCOTT JR.: PRAYER AND FASTING PIONEER
Compiled from many articles published by IFA over 50 years.
Photo credits: path at sunrise, Getty Images/Dave Alan; John Talcott at Plymouth's 350th anniversary celebration, John Talcott marching in a Plymouth parade, John Talcott leading an Annual Forefathers Day processional, John Talcott and Dr. Paul Jehle in top hats at Old Colony Club, John Talcott salutes Pilgrim Hall, Talcott in his 1909 Model T, John Talcott standing on

Pulpit Rock, John Talcott leading prayer at Pulpit Rock, all courtesy of Dr. Paul Jehle and the Plymouth Rock Foundation.

CHAPTER 25. MICHELLE GALLAGHER: MONUMENTAL PRAYERS
Originally published by IFA, May 2023.
Photo credits: Forefathers Monument in Plymouth, Massachusetts, courtesy of Sojourner Media, Plymouth, Massachusetts; *Forefathers Monument Guidebook,* courtesy of Proclamation House, Inc.; Forefathers Monument in Plymouth, Massachusetts, courtesy of Sojourner Media, Plymouth; Dan and Michelle Gallagher, Gallagher family private collection; Derek Prince, courtesy of Derek Prince Ministries; Billy Graham at Plymouth Rock, Billy Graham preaching at Memorial Hall in Plymouth, Digital Commonwealth, Brearley Collection, Boston Public Library, Creative Commons Attribution Non-Commercial No Derivatives License (CC BY-NC-ND); Forefathers Monument overlooking Plymouth Harbor, courtesy of Sojourner Media, Plymouth; *Monumental Prayers,* courtesy of Proclamation House, Inc.

CHAPTER 26. NANCY RIFE: 50 YEARS OF OBEDIENCE AND ENDURANCE
Photo credits: Explo '72 Photo@JP Laffont; Curt and Nancy Rife in 1973 and the late 2010s, VW bus, ocean baptism, Rife family collection; the Hotel Deauville, in Miami Beach, Florida. 1964, father-in-law of Timothy MN, CC BY-SA 4.0 https://creativecommons.org/licenses/by-sa/4.0, via Wikimedia Commons; hands outstretched over the horizon, Getty Images/BassittART; John Beckett with Nancy Rife, IFA archives.

CHAPTER 27. LT. COL. OLIVER NORTH: PRAYER FREED ME
Oliver North lives in Virginia with his wife of 56 years, Betsy. Originally published by IFA, April 2004. Excerpted with permission. *True Freedom,* by Lt. Col. Oliver North. His books are available at olivernorth.com.
Photo credits: Lt. Col. Oliver North testifies before Congress, Getty Images/Wally McNamee; UH-1D helicopters in Vietnam, 1966, James K.F. Dung, SFC, photographer, public domain, via Wikimedia Commons; Christmas services, Vietnam, December 1966 (11516100785), USMC archives from Quantico, USA, CC BY 2.0 https://creativecommons.org/licenses/by/2.0, via Wikimedia Commons; Assault Amphibious Vehicle, Getty Images/Stocktrek Images; soldier with Bible, Getty Images/BevLinder; President Ronald Reagan greeting Oliver North — Series: Reagan White House photographs, 1/20/1981– 1/20/1989 collection: White House photo collection, 1/20/1981–1/20/1989, public domain, via Wikimedia Commons; Oliver and Betsy North, Getty Images/Jemal Countess/staff; Oliver North visits Marines in Afghanistan 121012-M-EF955-034 — Sgt. Keonaona Paulo, public domain, via Wikimedia Commons.

CHAPTER 28. ANDREW BRUNSON: MISSIONARY DELIVERED FROM PRISON
Originally published by IFA, January 2019.
Photo credits: Pastor Brunson and his wife, Norine, prepare to leave Turkey, Getty Images/Bulent Kilic/contributor; God's Hostage, courtesy of Andrew Brunson; IFA staff with Andrew Brunson, IFA archives; Norine Brunson, Getty Images/Burak Kara/Stringer; President Erdogan, Getty Images/Defne Karadeniz/Stringer; convoy with Andrew Brunson, Getty Images/Chris McGrath/staff; Brunson prays for President Trump, Getty Images/Mark Wilson/staff; the Brunson family in the Oval Office, courtesy of CeCe Heil; hands clasped in prayer, Getty Images/NoonVirachada; secret Chinese church meeting, Getty Images/Jonathan Alpeyrie/contributor; Fana Tesema weeps, Getty Images/J. Countess/contributor; burned-out church building, Getty Images/Martyn Aim/contributor.